PURSUE Jesus, ***OBEY*** Jesus, ***LIVE*** for Jesus

Ann L. Knopp

ISBN 978-1-0980-9633-5 (paperback)
ISBN 978-1-0980-9634-2 (digital)

Copyright © 2021 by Ann L. Knopp

All rights reserved. No part of this publication may be reproduced, distributed, or transmitted in any form or by any means, including photocopying, recording, or other electronic or mechanical methods without the prior written permission of the publisher. For permission requests, solicit the publisher via the address below.

Christian Faith Publishing, Inc.
832 Park Avenue
Meadville, PA 16335
www.christianfaithpublishing.com

Printed in the United States of America

PURSUE

(Purposefully Understanding Our Risen Savior Until Eternity)

Book One

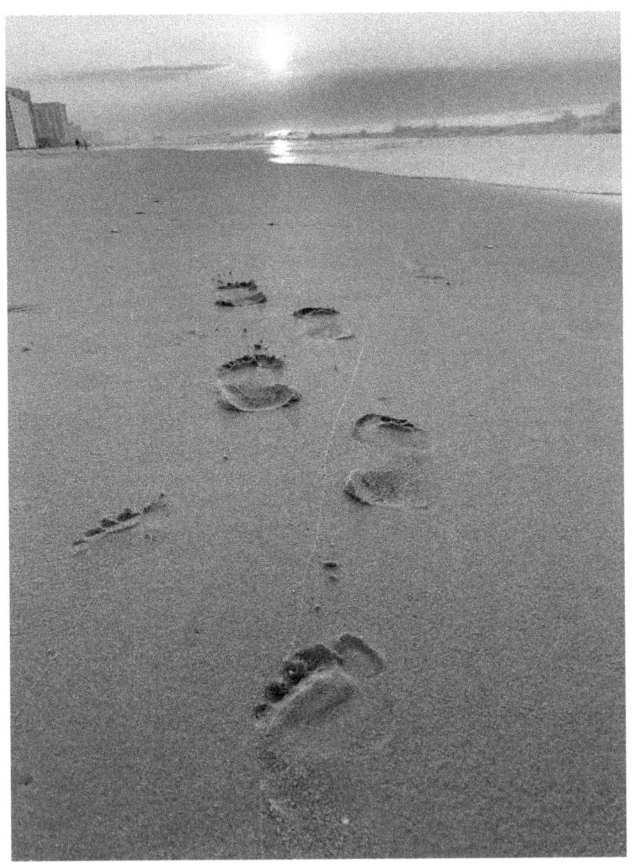

This photo by Ann L. Knopp is licensed under CC BY.

Table of Contents

Preface

My theme for 2017 was the word *pursue*. I wanted to pursue Christ Jesus with my whole being in every aspect of my life. I came up with an acrostic to model that desire.

Purposefully
Understanding our
Risen
Savior
Until
Eternity

Personally, I have always loved the examples set for us in Scripture for each aspect of our lives. In this book, we will break down a phrase or word each week. We will explore the good and bad decisions of biblical characters and how we can relate them to our decisions. The first three weeks, we will have the opportunity to look into the lives of these biblical characters, and then the last week, we will take the opportunity to put what we have learned into practice in our own lives.

Come join me on this journey as we *pursue* Jesus with a purpose and understanding, knowing fully that Christ is our alive and well-risen Savior and that we need to live for Him daily until we see Him again.

He is amazing, and we need to live in full pursuit of Him daily.

Thank you for choosing to pursue a deeper relationship with Christ through this Bible study/devotional. I am very excited to see what God can do through His words.

In Christ's love,
Ann Knopp

Week 1

Introduction: Why?

As adults, we have likely lost the enthusiasm and quick acceptance of anything. We are very often cynical, negative, and not always accepting of change.

Children, by contrast, can learn so much in a short amount of time. It is all so new and exciting. When Jesus says we are to "become as little children" (Matthew 18:3 NKJV), there are so many connotations to that. Come to Him with an innocence of mind, yet with every new experience, bring Him our questions and openness to hear the answers so that we can learn so much more. Come to Him as children and bring acceptance, curiosity, excitement, and a love for anything new that we can discover.

For this study, we need to get back to the age of curiosity, excitement, and an openness to receive without cynicism.

Children are also curious. They explore and inquire and ask. Their very favorite question seems to be, "Why?"

Why? That question has always intrigued me for the main reason that the more I ask why, the more why questions it creates. The beauty of why questions is that they generate such a learning time. That is the reason children are often encouraged to ask why, even if the chain of why questions does become somewhat tiresome to the person having to answer them all.

When we stop asking why, we are less pliable and moldable to God's plan and purpose for us. When we ask why, our mind stays open and able to receive all that is waiting. For this study, we need to ask the why questions as they apply to us.

> Ask and you will receive. Seek and you will find. Knock and the door will be opened. (Luke 11:9)

Never stop pursuing.

Day 1

What Does It Mean to Be Deliberate?

Francis Chan once said, "We never grow closer to God when we just live life. It takes deliberate pursuit and attentiveness."

As I looked up the definition of the word *deliberate*, I found that it meant done consciously or intentionally.

We have many examples in our lifetime of people that acted in a very deliberate manner in their pursuit, and in doing so, each of them made a lasting cultural impact for Christ. To name a few in recent years are Billy Graham, Jim and Elizabeth Elliott, Priscilla Shirer, Tim Tebow, and the list could go for books and books—not just of famous people but of anyone who committed his or her life to put Jesus first. Is it easy? No, but the rewards are heavenly.

Without the intentionality of seeking, we find nothing. There is a saying that goes, "Aim at nothing and you will hit it every time." I don't want to look back on my life and see that I have been living aimlessly without a purpose.

One afternoon at the seminary, I watched two brothers playing tag with a ball. The older brother ran free while the younger brother chased him with everything he had, trying to get close enough to hit him with the ball. Unfortunately, his little legs just weren't long enough to catch the older, bigger boy, but he pursued with gusto until finally he stopped and yelled for his brother to slow down. A few minutes later, big brother whizzed by on a scooter which made him even faster. Knowing that big brother would stop eventually, little brother kept running with the ball with full-blown determination that he would catch him. The younger brother eventually got his own scooter and waited until just the right moment. As the older brother passed by, he tagged him with the ball and rode happily along beside him.

Our pursuit should be just like the little brother: determined, never giving up, and eventually achieving success.

Read Philippians 3:12–14.

> Not that I have already obtained it or have already become perfect, but I press on so that I may lay hold of that for which also I was laid hold of by Christ Jesus. Brethren, I do not regard myself as having laid hold of it yet; but one thing I do: forgetting what lies behind and reaching forward to what lies ahead, I press on toward the goal for the prize of the upward call of God in Christ Jesus.

"As we are 'reaching forward to those things which are ahead,' there are obstacles in our path that can trip us up or slow us down. We face all kinds of challenges and trials. And to overcome those, we need the kind of driven focus Paul calls for in these verses—a focus that is repetitious in the sense that we keep keeping on. Our focus needs to be set on 1 Corinthians 10:31 that says, "Whether you eat or drink or whatever you do, do it all for the glory of God."

There is great value in determining your focus. When your goals are God's goals, you won't wander aimlessly through life and waste time and energy on fruitless pursuits. When you know exactly what to do, you'll make better choices and enjoy greater productivity. When the apostle Paul speaks of "reaching forward" in Philippians 3:13, he is describing himself as leaning toward the finish line, eyes fixed on the goal. He is devoting all his energy—mental, emotional, and physical—to running the straight path God has set before him. He doesn't step to the side or slow down. He is driven, motivated, and focused!

As Christians, God has given everything to us at our disposal because, after all, He does own the cattle on a thousand hills; we just need to use His resources. A. W. Tozer said, "It is a solemn thing, no small scandal in the kingdom, to see God's children starving while actually seated at the Father's table." Most people when they sit at a table for dinner, they eat. Christians are known to sit at the Father's table and not eat. It's time to eat! Take in all that God has for us and pursue Him with everything we have like the little boy chasing after his brother.

Question: What is holding you back from your pursuit of Jesus at this moment?

As Mel Gibson said in the movie, *The Patriot*, "Aim small, miss small." If our target is Jesus alone, we won't miss out on a life full and exciting. It's unlike anything we've ever dreamed of.

Day 2

The Woman Who Bled for Twelve Years

Read Mark 5:21–43.

When Jesus had crossed over again in the boat to the other side, a large crowd gathered around Him; and so He stayed by the seashore. One of the synagogue officials named Jairus came up, and on seeing Him, fell at His feet and implored Him earnestly, saying, "My little daughter is at the point of death; please come and lay Your hands on her, so that she will get well and live." And He went off with him; and a large crowd was following Him and pressing in on Him.

A woman who had had a hemorrhage for twelve years, and had endured much at the hands of many physicians, and had spent all that she had and was not helped at all, but rather had grown worse—after hearing about Jesus, she came up in the crowd behind Him and touched His cloak. For she thought, "If I just touch His garments, I will get well." Immediately the flow of her blood was dried up; and she felt in her body that she was healed of her affliction. Immediately Jesus, perceiving in Himself that the power proceeding from Him had gone forth, turned around in the crowd and said, "Who touched My garments?" And His disciples said to Him, "You see the crowd pressing in on You, and You say, 'Who touched Me?'" And He looked around to see the woman who had done this. But the woman fearing and trembling, aware of what had happened to her, came and fell down before Him and told Him the whole truth. And He said to her, "Daughter, your faith has made you well; go in peace and be healed of your affliction."

While He was still speaking, they came from the house of the synagogue official, saying, "Your daughter has died; why trouble the Teacher anymore?" But Jesus, overhearing what was being spoken, said to the synagogue official, "Do not be afraid any longer, only believe." And He allowed no one to accompany Him, except Peter and James and John the brother of James. They came to the house of the synagogue official; and He saw a commotion, and people loudly weeping and wailing. And entering in, He said to them, "Why make a commotion and weep? The child has not died, but is asleep." They began laughing at Him. But putting them all out, He took along the child's father and mother and His own companions, and entered the room where the child was. Taking the child by the hand, He said to her, "Talitha kum!" (which translated means, "Little girl, I say to you, get up!"). Immediately the girl got up and began to walk, for she was twelve years old. And immediately they were completely astounded. And He gave them strict orders that

> no one should know about this, and He said that something should be given her to eat.

There was a woman who had been bleeding (her monthly time) for twelve years without letup. Think about that. As women, our monthly time comes once a month for several days and then stops, and we are able to go about our lives until it comes around again. Pain (cramps) is but for a short time and then back to normal. This woman had pain and cramps for twelve years solid! Take into account that they didn't have feminine products back then and that creates a problem of being a social outcast because her clothes were always bloody and that would make her unclean in society.

On this particular morning, she had heard the news that Jesus was coming and she was at a desperate stage in her life. The pain was more than she could bear sometimes, and she was tired of living like she didn't have a purpose in society. So she set out to find Jesus in the midst of such a large, tight crowd who were also pushing their way toward Jesus.

She gritted her teeth and strained with everything she had and said, "If I can just touch the hem of his garment, I know that I can be healed." Just a touch is all it took. Her fingers barely grasped hold of the hem of his garment, and instantly, she felt His power rush through her, and the bleeding stopped.

At the exact same time, Jesus felt the power leave Him, and He stopped immediately and demanded to know who touched Him. The disciples were skeptical of His question because there were so many people pushing against Him, it could've been anyone. But Jesus knew it wasn't just anyone, and He also knew exactly who it was. She just had to stand and say, "It was me."

In order to get the full blessing of what God has for us, sometimes, we have to stand up and say, "It's me! I touched you! I need you!" We live with problems daily whether they be physical, mental, or emotional. Sometimes, God gives us our physical ailment so that through it, God is glorified and we can inspire others. Other times, God gives us ailments so that we can desperately run, kick, and shove our way to Jesus and let His healing power wash over us. There is a purpose for what God has given us in our lives. We must desperately pursue God in order to find out what it is. It says in Matthew 7:7, "Ask and it will be given, seek and you will find, knock and the door will be opened to you." If we don't seek, we won't find what we are looking for. If we don't knock, doors won't open. If we don't ask, answers will never be found. It is an active pursuit.

Question: What is stopping you from accessing answers that you seek?

Create a desperateness in the search for God because as they say in VBS Submerged 2016, "Jesus sees you, He knows you and He wants to save you." We just have to pursue Him with everything we have.

Day 3

Zacchaeus

Read Luke 19:1–10.

He entered Jericho and was passing through. And there was a man called by the name of Zacchaeus; he was a chief tax collector and he was rich. Zacchaeus was trying to see who Jesus was, and was unable because of the crowd, for he was small in stature. So he ran on ahead and climbed up into a sycamore tree in order to see Him, for He was about to pass through that way. When Jesus came to the place, He looked up and said to him, "Zacchaeus, hurry and come down, for today I must stay at your house." And he hurried and came down and received Him gladly. When they saw it, they all began to grumble, saying, "He has gone to be the guest of a man who is a sinner." Zacchaeus stopped and said to the Lord, "Behold, Lord, half of my possessions I will give to the poor, and if I have defrauded anyone of anything, I will give back four times as much." And Jesus said to him, "Today salvation has come to this house, because he, too, is a son

> of Abraham. For the Son of Man has come to seek and to save that which was lost."

We've all heard the song about Zacchaeus; at least that's what I thought until I taught third and fourth graders in Vacation Bible School. First of all, they had never heard of Zacchaeus, and second, if someone has never heard of him, then they definitely haven't heard the song about him, so I proceeded to teach them. The song goes like this: "Zacchaeus was a wee little man, and a wee little man was he. He climbed up in a sycamore tree for the Lord he wanted to see. As the Savior passed that way, He looked up in that tree. And he said, 'Zacchaeus! You come down! For I'm going to your house today. For I'm going to your house today.'"

If you know the song, it's going to be stuck in your head all day. You are welcome! Funny thing is, after teaching them the song, I would ask, "Who was Zacchaeus?" And they would scream out, "*A wee little man!*" That wasn't the point of the song, but they did remember who he was, and after several more questions, they also knew why he was important.

As I thought about people that would go well with my theme of pursuing Jesus, Zacchaeus popped into my mind, but I also thought him to be an odd choice until I started breaking down his story. Y'see, he wasn't an avid pursuer of Jesus, and I would say many of us are quite like him. He was very worldly, and to many, he was considered a thief just out for himself. But he was also very curious. Everyone had been talking about Jesus, so he knew he was coming to town. One thing you must know about Zacchaeus is that he was very short, so in large crowds, he just sort of disappeared. Instead of hiding in the shadows and observe, he went a step further and climbed a sycamore tree to be able to see and not be seen. So I will call him a curious pursuer.

Question: Have you ever been curious enough about God that you begin to read the Bible just enough to start to understand but you don't want God to change your life in any way? Or you might be afraid of what could happen that you have no control over?

Zacchaeus was the same way. He figured he would catch a glimpse of Jesus, and then when he passed by, he would go about his life as before. But that is not what happened. When we pursue Jesus, even if it is a bit reluctant, Jesus is pursuing us at the same time. Jesus walked by the tree, but he stopped. He looked up and called out saying, "Zacchaeus! Climb down out of the tree because I'm going to your house today." He not only noticed Zacchaeus who was hiding, He knew his name, He knew what he did for a living, but He also knew his future. The one everybody wanted to see, went, and spent time with the one, nobody wanted to see. Jesus said, "For the Son of Man came to seek and save that which was lost" (Luke 19:10). Jesus' desire is to save those which have not asked Jesus into their hearts because that is the only way to have Him come into their life.

Once we ask Him into our lives, that is the only way change occurs. That is exactly what happened with Zacchaeus. He immediately scampered down the tree and joined Jesus by His side. He didn't make up excuses as to why he should stay in the tree, he got down and went.

Question: If Jesus were walking by today and He looked at you square in the eye and said, "(input your name), climb down from your high perch and come follow Me," would you go or make excuses?

Once Zacchaeus let go of his excuses and joined Jesus at his house, Jesus was able to be real with him and change began to occur. Jesus told Zacchaeus things about himself that he didn't think anyone knew but him. As it was revealed, he realized that he couldn't live like that anymore.

When Jesus becomes our main pursuit, our desire for other things falls away. Zacchaeus became like Scrooge at the end of the Christmas Carol and declared that because of the immediate change in his life, "he was going to give half his possessions to the poor and if he cheated anyone out of anything, he would pay back 4x the amount" (Luke 19:8). Seeing the change not only on the outside but also on the inside, Jesus said, "Today, salvation has come to his house" (Luke 19:9).

Change of pursuit from our own wants to what God wants can sometimes be drastic or gradual, but when Jesus comes into our lives, rest assured, change will come!

Question: Are you ready to stop living for you and live for Jesus? He is waiting to go to your house; you just have to climb out of the tree.

Day 4

Mary and Martha

I've never really seen Mary and Martha as pursuers of Jesus but rather as planted by Him or around Him in some form or fashion. But I began to think toward the time when Lazarus died and they knew there was no one else who could possibly save him but it was too late—or was it? Now, I admit as most do, Martha takes a bad rap for the choices she made when she was around Jesus, but about a year ago, I realized it wasn't about the busyness that was the problem. It was that Jesus was there, in the house, at that time, for only a short time. She was so concerned with every need being met for everyone else that she missed the fact that her need for Jesus was being slighted. I learned this firsthand when friends of mine were in town and we had one hour to eat, fellowship, clean up, and go. So, while everyone was still eating and talking, I decided I would kill two birds with one stone by cleaning and semi-listening in order not to come back to a messy house. However, as they were talking, the laughter grew, and I found I couldn't hear the reason for all the laughter. God spoke to me right then saying, "You are Martha right now! Don't you see? Your friends are only here for a short time, and you are missing it! That's how it was with Martha. I was only there for a short time. She was concerned about being there for everyone, but she missed letting Me be there for her and rest in Me, even for just a little while." I finally understood and sat down to enjoy the rest of the evening.

The second time around of seeing Jesus was a bit more frantic, but Martha and Mary both knew where to go. However, their reactions were not the same, and even though the statement was the same for both, the intent behind them was different.

Question: When you ask questions of God, are they more accusing or more faith filled?

Read John 11:17–44.

> So, when Jesus came, He found that he had already been in the tomb four days. Now Bethany was near Jerusalem, about two miles off; and many of the Jews had come to Martha and Mary, to console them concerning their brother. Martha therefore, when she heard that Jesus was coming, went to meet Him, but Mary stayed at the house. Martha then said to Jesus, "Lord, if You had been here, my brother would not have died. Even now I know that whatever You ask of God, God will give You." Jesus said to her, "Your brother will rise again." Martha said to Him, "I know that he will rise again in the resurrection on the last day." Jesus said to her, "I am the resurrection and the life; he who believes in Me will live even if he dies, and everyone who lives and believes in Me will never die. Do you believe this?" She said to Him, "Yes, Lord; I have believed that You are the Christ, the Son of God, even He who comes into the world."
>
> When she had said this, she went away and called Mary her sister, saying secretly, "The Teacher is here and is calling for you." And when she heard it, she got up quickly and was coming to Him.
>
> Now Jesus had not yet come into the village, but was still in the place where Martha met Him.

Then the Jews who were with her in the house, and consoling her, when they saw that Mary got up quickly and went out, they followed her, supposing that she was going to the tomb to weep there. Therefore, when Mary came where Jesus was, she saw Him, and fell at His feet, saying to Him, "Lord, if You had been here, my brother would not have died." When Jesus therefore saw her weeping, and the Jews who came with her also weeping, He was deeply moved in spirit and was troubled, and said, "Where have you laid him?" They said to Him, "Lord, come and see." Jesus wept. So the Jews were saying, "See how He loved him!" But some of them said, "Could not this man, who opened the eyes of the blind man, have kept this man also from dying?"

So Jesus, again being deeply moved within, came to the tomb. Now it was a cave, and a stone was lying against it. Jesus said, "Remove the stone." Martha, the sister of the deceased, said to Him, "Lord, by this time there will be a stench, for he has been dead four days." Jesus said to her, "Did I not say to you that if you believe, you will see the glory of God?" So they removed the stone. Then Jesus raised His eyes, and said, "Father, I thank You that You have heard Me. "I knew that You always hear Me; but because of the people standing around I said it, so that they may believe that You sent Me." When He had said these things, He cried out with a loud voice, "Lazarus, come forth." The man who had died came forth, bound hand and foot with wrappings, and his face was wrapped around with a cloth. Jesus said to them, "Unbind him, and let him go."

Martha was a protector. After they sent word to Jesus about Lazarus dying, he came four days later, Martha's first reaction was, "Where were you? If you had been here my brother wouldn't have died!" (v. 21). Her reaction was full of hurt, anger, frustration, and overwhelming sadness. She knew what Jesus was capable of doing but couldn't fathom all that He was about to do. Jesus had to draw out of her that she believed in Him and who He was in order to show her that her belief needed to be stronger than the situation. He even asked her in verse 26, "If she believed that He was the resurrection and the life." I believe at that moment when she said, "Yes Lord, I believe," a peace that transcends all understanding fell over her to the point that she was able to leave His side and run to get Mary.

Mary, on the other hand, was in complete mourning and didn't go with Martha to see Jesus. But when Martha returned and said that the Teacher was asking for her, she didn't hesitate for a moment. She took off like lightning without saying a word to anyone which left them all wondering where she went. As soon as she got to Jesus, she fell at His feet and said the exact same thing that Martha said, but Jesus saw her heart and intent behind the statement. He didn't see accusation but rather faith and brokenness. This cut Jesus to the core because of His love for the family. He didn't have to ask if she believed for her sake of realization because He knew she knew. He simply said, "Where have you laid him?" (v. 34).

Question: Where is your faith in hard situations? Is it below the surface and the situation of worry taken over? Or is your faith so strong that all you have to do is ask and believe that what you ask will be handled in God's perfect will and timing without the worry?

Either way, God's power is amazing. Learn to trust, pursue Him, and then leave it there with Him to handle completely.

Day 5

The Blind Man Who Couldn't Be Silenced

Read Mark 10:46–52.

Then they came to Jericho. And as He was leaving Jericho with His disciples and a large crowd, a blind beggar named Bartimaeus, the son of Timaeus, was sitting by the road. When he heard that it was Jesus the Nazarene, he began to cry out and say, "Jesus, Son of David, have mercy on me!" Many were sternly telling him to be quiet, but he kept crying out all the more, "Son of David, have mercy on me!" And Jesus stopped and said, "Call him here." So, they called the blind man, saying to him, "Take courage, stand up! He is calling for you." Throwing aside his cloak, he jumped up and came to Jesus. And answering him, Jesus said, "What do you want Me to do for you?" And the blind man said to Him, "Rabboni, I want to regain my sight!" And Jesus said to him, "Go; your faith has made you well." Immediately he regained his sight and began following Him on the road.

There comes a time when sitting on the side of the road in our troubles becomes something we are tired of doing. At that time, we begin our search for answers to our dilemma. And not just search half-heartedly, no, we deliberately pursue an answer and set about changing our circumstances.

That's what the blind man was doing that day in Jerusalem. He got up from his bed, had his normal dark routine, and was taken to his place in the city to sit and beg for money or food. And then down the road came a man who would change his world forever. If I had been blind for all my life, one thing I would truly desire would be to see. Being dependent on others for everything every day of his life had to be depressing and exhausting not only to him but to those helping him every day.

When he heard Jesus coming, something stirred within him to do something. After all, he had been listening to people's conversations about Jesus for quite a while now. Sitting on the side of the road and listening to people talk, I'm sure he heard stories of healing, and from the healings, he heard joy, and lives changed. He desired that more than anything. So when Jesus came by, there was really no option. He had to get Jesus' attention so he too could have the healing and joy that he had heard from so many others.

Wherever Jesus went, there were throngs of people vying for his attention, and walking down this street was no different, so this blind man knew that he had to be incredibly loud to be noticed and he began to call out. The more he called out, the louder he became to the point of being obnoxious to the disciples. The disciples tried to keep him quiet and dissuade him from his pursuit.

Question: Have you known people that have tried to keep you from a change in your life? Have you been struggling for so long and finally found the solution in your walk with God and people just push you back down by telling you that your struggles aren't worth the Lord's trouble to help you?

I'm here to tell you that no matter how small the struggle or how big it is, Jesus takes notice and is ready and willing to change the circumstances. The key is despite the naysayers, we continue to cry out all the more. Our active pursuit of Christ for change will come.

As our pursuit of Him deepens, our passion changes. Our struggles become His struggles, and He lays on us His purpose for our lives which becomes the desire of our hearts (Psalm 37:4). This verse is not saying He will give us all our desires; its saying as we pursue Him, our desires change, and healing can begin.

Jesus took notice of the blind man's pursuit. He took notice of his belief. He took notice of the blind man, period. He knew the blind man. And with that, he was healed. Can you imagine never seeing and the first face you do see is Jesus? Wow!

Question: What are you struggling with these days that you are tired of dealing with?

Take it to Jesus, leave it at His feet. Actually, call out to Him until all the naysayers fade into the background and all we hear is Jesus say, "Come to Me, all who are weary and I will give you rest" (Matthew 11:28). "Let Me take your struggles and I will change your world!" What are we waiting for?

Week 2

Introduction: Why Is It Important to Understand God's Instructions?

Knowing directions correctly is critical in getting where we are going in a timely fashion. Prime example of this is when we were going to my brother's new house for the first time with my parents. I guess general questions were asked about where on this road he lived, but all the directions got mixed up in translation, and we ended up in a completely different place only to find out we went two mountains and fifteen miles further than we should've. The problem with getting lost on a mountain is that there is no cell phone service, so we couldn't even call for help. On top of that, no one remembered to bring the house number to aid in the search. On the way back down one of the mountains, I looked over and noticed an open gate and asked if they had a gate. Dad took a chance, turned around, and drove through the gate to discover that we had indeed found their home.

Our lives lived in God's plan are completely laid out for us. The directions for some were step-by-step, and some were given directions as they went along. The key to getting instructions from God was that the communication lines were never broken, and as long as they followed the instructions, then all went well, and God was glorified. It's when they veered off the path that trouble came. Thankfully,

God's plans and forgiveness are broader than our box that we live in. In the end, God will receive the victory.

This week, we will study about five people that received their instructions from God, how they followed them, what became of the end result, and what we can take away from it and use in our own lives.

Day 1

Adam

Read Genesis 2.

Thus, the heavens and the earth were completed in all their vast array.

By the seventh day God had finished the work he had been doing; so on the seventh day he rested from all his work. Then God blessed the seventh day and made it holy, because on it he rested from all the work of creating that he had done.

This is the account of the heavens and the earth when they were created, when the LORD God made the earth and the heavens.

Now no shrub had yet appeared on the earth and no plant had yet sprung up, for the LORD God had not sent rain on the earth and there was no one to work the ground, but streams came up from the earth and watered the whole surface of the ground. Then the LORD God formed a man from the dust of the ground and breathed into his nostrils the breath of life, and the man became a living being.

Now the LORD God had planted a garden in the east, in Eden; and there he put the man he had formed. The LORD God made all kinds of trees grow out of the ground—trees that were pleasing to the eye and good for food. In the middle of the garden were the tree of life and the tree of the knowledge of good and evil.

A river watering the garden flowed from Eden; from there it was separated into four headwaters. The name of the first is the Pishon; it winds through the entire land of Havilah, where there is gold. (The gold of that land is good; aromatic resin and onyx are also there.) The name of the second river is the Gihon; it winds through the entire land of Cush. The name of the third river is the Tigris; it runs along the east side of Ashur. And the fourth river is the Euphrates.

The LORD God took the man and put him in the Garden of Eden to work it and take care of it. And the LORD God commanded the man, "You are free to eat from any tree in the garden; but you must not eat from the tree of the knowledge of good and evil, for when you eat from it you will certainly die."

The LORD God said, "It is not good for the man to be alone. I will make a helper suitable for him."

Now the LORD God had formed out of the ground all the wild animals and all the birds in the sky. He brought them to the man to see what he would name them; and whatever the man called each living creature, that was its name. So the man gave names to all the livestock, the birds in the sky and all the wild animals.

But for Adam no suitable helper was found. So the LORD God caused the man to fall into

> a deep sleep; and while he was sleeping, he took one of the man's ribs and then closed up the place with flesh. Then the LORD God made a woman from the rib he had taken out of the man, and he brought her to the man.
>
> The man said, "This is now bone of my bones and flesh of my flesh; she shall be called 'woman,' for she was taken out of man." That is why a man leaves his father and mother and is united to his wife, and they become one flesh.
>
> Adam and his wife were both naked, and they felt no shame.

Adam had a rare relationship with God that no one else has ever had. He was the first man that God created. He and Eve were also the only two humans ever created without a sin nature. God gave very detailed instructions on how to rule over the garden of Eden. He told Adam that "everything was his to enjoy EXCEPT for the tree of knowledge of good and evil. Of that tree he was not allowed to eat and if he did then he would die" (2:17). Seems pretty simple and straight forward, doesn't it? But it's like saying to a child, don't touch the stove because it's hot and they try to touch it to see if what you say is true. Most of the time, the end result was burned fingers or a slap on the hand, pain either way. But curiosity didn't come for him the way it comes for us.

All was fine, and I really think Adam didn't think another thing about the tree because God kept him busy about the work of naming the animals and plants and basically everything created. You see, when we are about the business that God sets in front of us, we don't have time to wander in thought or action. Once his tasks were done, then God saw that nothing in creation was a suitable companion, so He created Eve from Adam. This is when things began to change. When Eve was created, trouble didn't immediately start. The reason I know this is because Eve knew the rules. Adam probably introduced her to all the animals and told her the main instructions of the garden. They both understood it and lived in peace because their focus was not on them. They probably carried on conversations with animals because when Eve was approached by a talking serpent, there was no fear. It seemed like a normal occurrence. Sadly, it was not.

Read Genesis 3.

> Now the serpent was more crafty than any of the wild animals the LORD God had made. He said to the woman, "Did God really say, 'You must not eat from any tree in the garden'?"
>
> The woman said to the serpent, "We may eat fruit from the trees in the garden, but God did say, 'You must not eat fruit from the tree that is in the middle of the garden, and you must not touch it, or you will die.'"
>
> "You will not certainly die," the serpent said to the woman. "For God knows that when you eat from it your eyes will be opened, and you will be like God, knowing good and evil."
>
> When the woman saw that the fruit of the tree was good for food and pleasing to the eye, and also desirable for gaining wisdom, she took some and ate it. She also gave some to her husband, who was with her, and he ate it. Then the eyes of both of them were opened, and they realized they were naked; so they sewed fig leaves together and made coverings for themselves.
>
> Then the man and his wife heard the sound of the LORD God as he was walking in the garden in the cool of the day, and they hid from the LORD God among the trees of the garden. But the LORD God called to the man, "Where are you?"
>
> He answered, "I heard you in the garden, and I was afraid because I was naked; so I hid."

And he said, "Who told you that you were naked? Have you eaten from the tree that I commanded you not to eat from?"

The man said, "The woman you put here with me—she gave me some fruit from the tree, and I ate it."

Then the LORD God said to the woman, "What is this you have done?"

The woman said, "The serpent deceived me, and I ate."

So the LORD God said to the serpent, "Because you have done this, Cursed are you above all livestock and all wild animals! You will crawl on your belly and you will eat dust all the days of your life. And I will put enmity between you and the woman, and between your offspring and hers; he will crush your head, and you will strike his heel."

To the woman he said, "I will make your pains in childbearing very severe; with painful labor you will give birth to children. Your desire will be for your husband, and he will rule over you."

To Adam he said, "Because you listened to your wife and ate fruit from the tree about which I commanded you, 'You must not eat from it,' Cursed is the ground because of you; through painful toil you will eat food from it all the days of your life. It will produce thorns and thistles for you, and you will eat the plants of the field. By the sweat of your brow you will eat your food until you return to the ground, since from it you were taken; for dust you are and to dust you will return."

Adam named his wife Eve, because she would become the mother of all the living.

> The LORD God made garments of skin for Adam and his wife and clothed them. And the LORD God said, "The man has now become like one of us, knowing good and evil. He must not be allowed to reach out his hand and take also from the tree of life and eat, and live forever." So the LORD God banished him from the Garden of Eden to work the ground from which he had been taken. After he drove the man out, he placed on the east side of the Garden of Eden cherubim and a flaming sword flashing back and forth to guard the way to the tree of life.

Satan is very cunning and crafty and uses words against us on many occasions. He will twist just one word or two to make it sound similar and almost correct and then twist it again to make us think that what we are thinking is wrong. He did that with Adam and Eve. Now remember, God told Adam the rules of the garden which was simply, "Don't eat of the tree of knowledge of good and evil or when you eat of it you will surely die" (2:17). Then Adam passed along the same information to Eve. We assume it was not passed down correctly because when she told the serpent, she added some information that God didn't say. She said, "You must not eat fruit from the tree in the middle of the Garden and you must not touch it or you will surely die" (3:3).

Question: Have you ever played the gossip game? By the time we have whispered the message from one person to another to another, etc., the message sounds nothing like we heard at the beginning.

It was the same with Eve. She was getting hearsay from Adam then added an extra touch to the rules. Here's the problem: Adam was standing right beside her and never corrected her statement. He stood as a silent sideline observer until it was time to participate.

As soon as Satan heard the new version to the garden rules, he knew he could manipulate Eve and proceeded to weave doubt and curiosity into a life that lacked nothing. They had it all! No care in the world and the ultimate freedom, and yet since Satan couldn't have it, he didn't want anyone else to have it. At one time, Satan was the head angel and the most beautiful, but it wasn't enough. He wanted to be God. There can only be one God, and he was not it, so God banished him from heaven to live on Earth. So he planted in the minds of Adam and Eve that what they had wasn't enough. Not knowing any better, their curiosity was piqued and desire for more crept in. They both ate—Eve then Adam—then their eyes were opened to everything. The very first thing that happened was shame filled their minds and they hid from God.

Several things happened quickly after that:

- God came looking for them and, when found, asked them why they were hiding. (God already knew, but He needed them to admit to their sin.) They were honest to tell Him what happened.
- God's instructions changed, not only for Adam and Eve but also for the creatures and plants and all creation, especially the serpent.
- Then God spoke with Himself and knew that since Adam and Eve now held the knowledge that God had, they couldn't live forever and had to be taken out of the garden and away from the tree of life.

How do we apply this to our life?

- God gives us instructions to follow, and it is important that we understand them correctly and not add to or take away.
- Consequences come as a result of change.
- God sees the ultimate picture, so it just makes sense to leave His instructions as is and then follow them. Peace and contentment will have amazing impacts on our lives because of it.

Day 2

Abram/Abraham

Read Genesis 12:1–6.

Now the LORD said to Abram, "Go forth from your country, and from your relatives and from your father's house, to the land which I will show you; and I will make you a great nation, and I will bless you, and make your name great; and so you shall be a blessing; and I will bless those who bless you, and the one who curses you I will curse. And in you all the families of the earth will be blessed."

So Abram went forth as the LORD had spoken to him; and Lot went with him. Now Abram was seventy-five years old when he departed from Haran. Abram took Sarai his wife and Lot his nephew, and all their possessions which they had accumulated, and the persons which they had acquired in Haran, and they set out for the land of Canaan; thus they came to the land of Canaan. Abram passed through the land as far as the site of Shechem, to the oak of Moreh. Now the Canaanite was then in the land.

"Leave your country, your people and your father's household and go to the land I will show you" (12:1). "So Abram left as the Lord told him" (12:4a). It was one simple instruction, no fanfare, and no long explanation of the necessity for moving. Basically, God simply said, "Go." Abram didn't ask questions, he didn't protest, he simply went. It seems too easy. It really wasn't a pack a bag and go on vacation. It was pack up your life along with all the family and livestock and leave together. I have always wondered if anyone protested or questioned the craziness of the move because think about it, God said, "Leave your country…and I will show you where to go" (12:1). There was no itinerary, no timeline of things to see on the journey. It was pure faith.

I must say, in all my years of moving from place to place, I ask a lot of question. Will we have enough money to live on? Are we sure we want to do this? Are we sure God is calling us to go? Not until questions have satisfying answers do I say, "If God is in it, let's go." Yet we don't hear that from Abram or Sarai or Lot or Terah or anyone! They just went.

Read Genesis 12:10–20.

> Now there was a famine in the land; so Abram went down to Egypt to sojourn there, for the famine was severe in the land. It came about when he came near to Egypt, that he said to Sarai his wife, "See now, I know that you are a beautiful woman; and when the Egyptians see you, they will say, 'This is his wife'; and they will kill me, but they will let you live. Please say that you are my sister so that it may go well with me because of you, and that I may live on account of you." It came about when Abram came into Egypt, the Egyptians saw that the woman was very beautiful. Pharaoh's officials saw her and praised her to Pharaoh; and the woman was taken into Pharaoh's house. Therefore, he treated Abram well for her sake; and gave him sheep and

> oxen and donkeys and male and female servants and female donkeys and camels.
>
> But the LORD struck Pharaoh and his house with great plagues because of Sarai, Abram's wife. Then Pharaoh called Abram and said, "What is this you have done to me? Why did you not tell me that she was your wife? Why did you say, 'She is my sister,' so that I took her for my wife? Now then, here is your wife, take her and go." Pharaoh commanded his men concerning him; and they escorted him away, with his wife and all that belonged to him.

It is interesting to note that along their journey, Abram's faith gave way to doubt, and he took matters into his own hands not once but twice. The first time was when they were in Egypt. They met up with Pharaoh in Egypt, and they played Sarai off as his sister to save them from death. Thankfully, God still had amazing plans for Abram and Sarai, so He struck Pharaoh and his house with a plague. Seeing what was going on, Pharaoh knew that Abram was God's man and gave Sarai back as well as servants and cattle. So despite their lack of faith for the moment, God blessed them.

Then the Lord promised Abram offspring in Genesis 13:15–16, 15:5. However, he and Sarai were getting up in age, past childbearing years, and still no child. So instead of trusting in the Lord's Word and His perfect timing, Abram began listening to the voice of his wife, Sarai. She started giving him "logical" advice in Genesis 16:2. "The Lord has kept me from having children, go sleep with my maidservant and I can build a family through her. So Abram agreed." Abram didn't consult God on this one, and thus, trouble began. *Read all Genesis 16 for the full story.* Long story short, Hagar had a son, and jealousy reared its ugly head to the point that Hagar ran away. God told her to go back. After Isaac finally was born in Genesis 21, jealousy between half-brothers grew. Sarah wanted Hagar banished and asked Abraham to agree. This time, Abraham learned his lesson and sought God's guidance instead of Sarah's.

I can see Abraham's faith grow stronger with each act of faith he had to take. I guess that is why he is known as the Father of our faith. We've seen him walk out in faith in leaving his country and then fall when he went on his own, and then in the ultimate act of faith of sacrificing his son, he didn't ask questions; he just went. He knew God's promise to him of having offspring as much as the dust of the earth, so if he were to sacrifice his only son, he knew God would provide another in his place.

Read Genesis 22:1–18.

> "Now it came about after these things, that God tested Abraham, and said to him, "Abraham!" And he said, "Here I am." He said, "Take now your son, your only son, whom you love, Isaac, and go to the land of Moriah, and offer him there as a burnt offering on one of the mountains of which I will tell you." So, Abraham rose early in the morning and saddled his donkey, and took two of his young men with him and Isaac his son; and he split wood for the burnt offering, and arose and went to the place of which God had told him. On the third day Abraham raised his eyes and saw the place from a distance. Abraham said to his young men, "Stay here with the donkey, and I and the lad will go over there; and we will worship and return to you." Abraham took the wood of the burnt offering and laid it on Isaac his son, and he took in his hand the fire and the knife. So the two of them walked on together. Isaac spoke to Abraham his father and said, "My father!" And he said, "Here I am, my son." And he said, "Behold, the fire and the wood, but where is the lamb for the burnt offering?" Abraham said, "God will provide for

> Himself the lamb for the burnt offering, my son." So, the two of them walked on together.
>
> Then they came to the place of which God had told him; and Abraham built the altar there and arranged the wood, and bound his son Isaac and laid him on the altar, on top of the wood. Abraham stretched out his hand and took the knife to slay his son. But the angel of the LORD called to him from heaven and said, "Abraham, Abraham!" And he said, "Here I am." He said, "Do not stretch out your hand against the lad, and do nothing to him; for now, I know that you fear God, since you have not withheld your son, your only son, from Me." Then Abraham raised his eyes and looked, and behold, behind him a ram caught in the thicket by his horns; and Abraham went and took the ram and offered him up for a burnt offering in the place of his son. Abraham called the name of that place The LORD Will Provide, as it is said to this day, "In the mount of the LORD it will be provided."
>
> Then the angel of the LORD called to Abraham a second time from heaven, and said, "By Myself I have sworn, declares the LORD, because you have done this thing and have not withheld your son, your only son, indeed I will greatly bless you, and I will greatly multiply your seed as the stars of the heavens and as the sand which is on the seashore; and your seed shall possess the gate of their enemies. In your seed all the nations of the earth shall be blessed, because you have obeyed My voice."

God said, "Take your son and sacrifice him… Abraham got up the next morning and took his son and two servants with him to the region of Moriah." It was only Isaac that asked where the sacrifice was to be burned. All Abraham said was, "God will provide" (22:8). That was all Isaac asked, and that's all Abraham offered. I don't know about anyone else, but if I began to be wrapped with rope and put on an altar, I would ask more questions or at least protest. And he might've, but nothing is written. Thankfully, as he was about to sacrifice Isaac, the Lord called out to stop. Lo and behold, the provided sacrifice was caught in the thicket. The sacrifice was made, and a promise of a future was given by the Lord.

How do we apply this to our life?

- Abram/Abraham had unshakable faith but only when he started listening to the wrong voices did things go astray.
- Sometimes, God will give us instructions for our future that won't happen for years to come. Know that God is faithful to fulfill His promises, we just have to be faithful to wait. And once His promises are fulfilled in us, we need to recognize and give Him honor and praise for it all.

Day 3

Lot's Wife

"Remember Lot's wife. Whoever seeks to keep his life shall lose it and whoever loses his life shall preserve it" (Luke 17:32–33). For someone whose name is not important to remember, she has a big impact in the Bible for what *not* to do. God gave specific instructions to follow, and Lot's wife just couldn't follow them therefore leading to her destruction.

Let's go back a bit to where she comes into the picture. The Bible doesn't say where Lot's wife came from, but by the time the angels came to visit Lot, he is married and has two daughters. Lot started with Abraham, and in Genesis 13:6–11, their herdsmen started fighting, so Abraham gave Lot first choice on where to live. Naturally, he chose the land that was plusher and primed for success. This also allowed him to live near Sodom which was a very wicked city.

Read Genesis 14.

> And it came about in the days of Amraphel king of Shinar, Arioch king of Ellasar, Chedorlaomer king of Elam, and Tidal king of Goiim, that they made war with Bera king of Sodom, and with Birsha king of Gomorrah, Shinab king of Admah, and Shemeber king of Zeboiim, and the king of Bela (that is, Zoar). All

these came as allies to the valley of Siddim (that is, the Salt Sea). Twelve years they had served Chedorlaomer, but the thirteenth year they rebelled. In the fourteenth year Chedorlaomer and the kings that were with him, came and defeated the Rephaim in Ashteroth-karnaim and the Zuzim in Ham and the Emim in Shaveh-kiriathaim, and the Horites in their Mount Seir, as far as El-paran, which is by the wilderness. Then they turned back and came to En-mishpat (that is, Kadesh), and conquered all the country of the Amalekites, and also the Amorites, who lived in Hazazon-tamar. And the king of Sodom and the king of Gomorrah and the king of Admah and the king of Zeboiim and the king of Bela (that is, Zoar) came out; and they arrayed for battle against them in the valley of Siddim, against Chedorlaomer king of Elam and Tidal king of Goiim and Amraphel king of Shinar and Arioch king of Ellasar—four kings against five. Now the valley of Siddim was full of tar pits; and the kings of Sodom and Gomorrah fled, and they fell into them. But those who survived fled to the hill country. Then they took all the goods of Sodom and Gomorrah and all their food supply, and departed. They also took Lot, Abram's nephew, and his possessions and departed, for he was living in Sodom.

Then a fugitive came and told Abram the Hebrew. Now he was living by the oaks of Mamre the Amorite, brother of Eshcol and brother of Aner, and these were allies with Abram. When Abram heard that his relative had been taken captive, he led out his trained men, born in his house, three hundred and eighteen, and went in pursuit as far as Dan. He divided his forces against them

> by night, he and his servants, and defeated them, and pursued them as far as Hobah, which is north of Damascus. He brought back all the goods, and also brought back his relative Lot with his possessions, and also the women, and the people.
>
> Then after his return from the defeat of Chedorlaomer and the kings who were with him, the king of Sodom went out to meet him at the valley of Shaveh (that is, the King's Valley). And Melchizedek king of Salem brought out bread and wine; now he was a priest of God Most High.
>
> He blessed him and said, "Blessed be Abram of God Most High, Possessor of heaven and earth; And blessed be God Most High, who has delivered your enemies into your hand." He gave him a tenth of all.
>
> The king of Sodom said to Abram, "Give the people to me and take the goods for yourself." Abram said to the king of Sodom, "I have sworn to the LORD God Most High, possessor of heaven and earth, that I will not take a thread or a sandal thong or anything that is yours, for fear you would say, 'I have made Abram rich.' I will take nothing except what the young men have eaten, and the share of the men who went with me, Aner, Eshcol, and Mamre; let them take their share."

"Lot was no longer *near* Sodom but living *in* Sodom" (v. 21). He was actually living out Psalm 1:1: "Blessed is the man who does not walk in the counsel of the wicked, or stand in the way of sinners or sit in the seat of mockers." He did all that. First, he saw what was pleasing to the eye and went in that direction, then he began to live *near* Sodom to be close but not fully invested. Then he gave in and chose to live *in* the city of wickedness. It is so easy to get involved in something that we shouldn't if our delight is not in the Lord (Psalm 1:2).

Choices ultimately make or break us. Bad decisions lead to bad circumstances. Knowing that Lot and his family were living *in* Sodom means that they weren't concerned for what God would have for them rather what they could get for themselves. Lot's wife *loved* Sodom, and when the angels told Lot and his family to leave and never look back, he hesitated. Then angels had to literally pull them out of the city. I must admit, there have been places I have lived that I loved with my whole heart from my home to the people to the church to the city—I loved it all. I hated to leave and found myself going back time and time again to reminisce or relive old memories. You know what I discovered? It wasn't the same place anymore. The place had changed. The people didn't mourn my absence; they went on about their lives, and I found myself longing for where I was living and ready to move on. Lot's wife was similar but different. I would guess she left with a bit of a kick and a scream and a desire to stay. Thus, when she saw the fire and brimstone go over her head toward Sodom, it was just a natural instinct to look back and take in what was happening. Sort of reminds me of rubberneckers on the highway, always stopping to check out the wreck on the side of the road.

Lot's wife wanted the things of this world, and Jesus said, "Whoever seeks to keep his/her old life will lose it, but whoever loses his/her old life for My sake will find it." Choices will make or break us. Do we want to be broken under God's judgment, or do we want to be molded under God's love and mercy? It's a simple decision, or is it?

How do we apply this to our life?

- Make the right choices under God's guidance.
- Be moldable rather than breakable.

Day 4

Shadrach, Meshach, and Abednego

Read Daniel 3.

King Nebuchadnezzar made an image of gold, sixty cubits high and six cubits wide, and set it up on the plain of Dura in the province of Babylon. He then summoned the satraps, prefects, governors, advisers, treasurers, judges, magistrates, and all the other provincial officials to come to the dedication of the image he had set up. So the satraps, prefects, governors, advisers, treasurers, judges, magistrates, and all the other provincial officials assembled for the dedication of the image that King Nebuchadnezzar had set up, and they stood before it.

Then the herald loudly proclaimed, "Nations and peoples of every language, this is what you are commanded to do. As soon as you hear the sound of the horn, flute, zither, lyre, harp, pipe, and all kinds of music, you must fall down and worship the image of gold that King Nebuchadnezzar has set up. Whoever does not fall down and worship will immediately be thrown into a blazing furnace."

Therefore, as soon as they heard the sound of the horn, flute, zither, lyre, harp, and all kinds of music, all the nations and peoples of every language fell down and worshiped the image of gold that King Nebuchadnezzar had set up.

At this time, some astrologers came forward and denounced the Jews. They said to King Nebuchadnezzar, "May the king live forever! Your Majesty has issued a decree that everyone who hears the sound of the horn, flute, zither, lyre, harp, pipe, and all kinds of music must fall down and worship the image of gold, and that whoever does not fall down and worship will be thrown into a blazing furnace. But there are some Jews whom you have set over the affairs of the province of Babylon—Shadrach, Meshach, and Abednego—who pay no attention to you, Your Majesty. They neither serve your gods nor worship the image of gold you have set up."

Furious with rage, Nebuchadnezzar summoned Shadrach, Meshach, and Abednego. So these men were brought before the king, and Nebuchadnezzar said to them, "Is it true, Shadrach, Meshach, and Abednego, that you do not serve my gods or worship the image of gold I have set up? Now when you hear the sound of the horn, flute, zither, lyre, harp, pipe, and all kinds of music, if you are ready to fall down and worship the image I made, very good. But if you do not worship it, you will be thrown immediately into a blazing furnace. Then what god will be able to rescue you from my hand?"

Shadrach, Meshach, and Abednego replied to him, "King Nebuchadnezzar, we do not need to defend ourselves before you in this matter. If we are thrown into the blazing furnace, the God we serve is able to deliver us from it, and he will deliver us from Your Majesty's hand. But even if he does not, we want you to know, Your Majesty, that we will not serve your gods or worship the image of gold you have set up."

Then Nebuchadnezzar was furious with Shadrach, Meshach, and Abednego, and his attitude toward them changed. He ordered the furnace heated seven times hotter than usual and commanded some of the strongest soldiers in his army to tie up Shadrach, Meshach, and Abednego and throw them into the blazing furnace. So these men—wearing their robes, trousers, turbans, and other clothes—were bound and thrown into the blazing furnace. The king's command was so urgent and the furnace so hot that the flames of the fire killed the soldiers who took up Shadrach, Meshach, and Abednego, and these three men—firmly tied—fell into the blazing furnace.

Then King Nebuchadnezzar leaped to his feet in amazement and asked his advisers, "Weren't there three men that we tied up and threw into the fire?"

They replied, "Certainly, Your Majesty."

He said, "Look! I see four men walking around in the fire, unbound and unharmed, and the fourth looks like a son of the gods."

Nebuchadnezzar then approached the opening of the blazing furnace and shouted, "Shadrach, Meshach, and Abednego, servants of the Most High God, come out! Come here!"

So Shadrach, Meshach, and Abednego came out of the fire, and the satraps, prefects, governors, and royal advisers crowded around them. They saw that the fire had not harmed their

> bodies nor was a hair of their heads singed; their robes were not scorched, and there was no smell of fire on them.
>
> Then Nebuchadnezzar said, "Praise be to the God of Shadrach, Meshach, and Abednego, who has sent his angel and rescued his servants! They trusted in him and defied the king's command and were willing to give up their lives rather than serve or worship any god except their own God. Therefore, I decree that the people of any nation or language who say anything against the God of Shadrach, Meshach, and Abednego be cut into pieces and their houses be turned into piles of rubble, for no other god can save in this way."
>
> Then the king promoted Shadrach, Meshach, and Abednego in the province of Babylon.

Peer pressure is a hard thing to say no to sometimes, especially if we are the only one standing up for what we believe. Take Rachel Scott from Columbine. She stood up for her belief and said that she was not ashamed of the Gospel of Christ. It cost her her life, but that did not deter her from saying, "Yes, I believe." There are so many others that stand up for what they believe, and people are killed for it daily. Are all people killed for their beliefs? No, otherwise, I wouldn't be writing this. But those that take a stand in the midst of extreme pressure are examples for us to follow. Paul said, "Either I live for Christ or I die for Christ, but either way, I see Jesus." It may be today or when I'm old, but we gain Jesus either way. To live for Christ in the midst of peer pressure means we understand what God is calling us to do for Him. Shadrach, Meshach, and Abednego stood up for what they believed, but they understood that following what God said to do had a cost that went with it and they were willing to pay that price.

Shadrach, Meshach, and Abednego were teenage boys being trained in the army of the king during the reign of King Nebuchadnezzar. The king had some bad advisors and a huge ego. The king and his advisors didn't like the three teenage boys because they held God to a higher respect than the king. So the advisors came up with a plan that everyone would bow down to an idol of the king's image every day, or they would be thrown into the fiery furnace. They knew that would help eliminate their issue of the boys because either they bowed down and in turn renounce God as king or be thrown into the furnace. Either way, they win. But God had other plans.

When God has a plan and we understand and follow His plan, the plan will work as it should, and God will be glorified, which is what our lives are all about anyway: glorifying God. This situation was no different. These teenage boys understood what they were supposed to do even if it cost them their lives and they set out to do it together. In Ecclesiastes 4:12, it says a cord of three cannot be broken (and in this case, four). If we stand alone, people have an easier time of tearing us down, and we fall. Even if there are two of us, it's hard. But the more that stand together, it's easier to stand firm. Then when we add God into the mix and He is standing with us, it becomes an ultimate victory.

The day Shadrach, Meshach, and Abednego refused to bow down was a monumental day that changed many, many lives. I can just imagine the advisors were almost giddy because they were finally going to get rid of these boys that I'm sure were liked by so many. The fire was so hot that day, and they had made sure it was extra hot so that it wouldn't take long for them to die. In fact, it was so hot that when the soldiers took them to the furnace, they were the ones that died instead because they got too close. The boys walked in and closed the door. The king looked in and asked, "Didn't we just put in three men? Why are there four standing in there?" God had sent one of His angels (some believe it was Jesus) to stand in the fire with them. The king brought them out, and only three came out, unsinged and totally unharmed. From that day forward, the king decreed that everyone would worship their God.

God will walk through the fire with us. He will stand in the fire with us. We just have to understand, believe, and commit ourselves to His ways.

Question: What are you struggling to stand up against but are willing to do because you know that God is standing beside you?

Day 5

The Greatest Commandment/ Great Commission

Jesus was our greatest instruction giver when it comes to those in human form. God is ultimate, but then again, Jesus is God, so it stands to reason why He would be the ultimate instruction giver. But He not only gave instructions, but also He lived out the example of the instructions. What a joy and a blessing! We are just going to focus on three instructions today because they are the greatest instructions for our lives to follow on a daily basis.

Read Matthew 22:37–39.

> And He said to him, "'You shall love the Lord your God with all your heart, and with all your soul, and with all your mind.' "This is the great and foremost commandment. "The second is like it, 'You shall love your neighbor as yourself.'"

Jesus had been constantly badgered by the Pharisees and Sadducees (leaders in the community). They decided to test Him one more time by asking Him what the greatest commandment was in the Law. Jesus said, "Love the Lord your God with all your heart, soul and mind. And then love your neighbor as yourself. All the law and the prophets hang on these two commandments."

It's simple really: love God and love people. Love God first, and if He is truly first in our life, loving people will be a natural progression in our life. The Ten Commandments were based on these two commandments. The first four commandments deal with putting God first and loving Him fully. The next six commandments are how to interact and love people.

If we follow these two great commandments, our lives may not be easy, but the priorities will be in order, and then He can do amazing things in and through us. It took a weekend of priority rearranging to get to where God could take me on an amazing journey of life I would've never seen without Him being first in my life. Because of that day, I am married to a fabulous man of God, have two amazing sons that are growing in God's grace daily, and I get to minister to whoever I come in contact with and know that God put them in my life to love. So I do.

Before Jesus left this earth for the last time, He gave one final instruction: "Go, therefore and make disciples of all nations, baptizing them in the name of the Father, the Son and the Holy Spirit. Teaching them to obey all I have commanded you and lo (*behold!*), I am with you always, even to the end of the age" (Matthew 28:19–20).

There is something to be said about the Greek language because it truly sets a tone for the underlying intent of what was truly being said by Jesus that day. Jesus said, "Go!" This was not a go if we want to. It was not a go tomorrow after we've slept in. It was not a request at all! It was a command. But it was not a go to places we've never been and leave everything behind (for some it might be). Jesus' command of "go" was, "As we are going, make disciples." That means when we are at home, make disciples of our children. When we are at work, show them Jesus in our lives. When we are at the grocery store, be the only Jesus they might see that day. As we are going, love God, love our neighbor, and tell people about Jesus. In the end, God will ultimately be glorified, and that is why we are made for this earth anyway. And that is to glorify Him in all we say and do.

Question: Where are you going today that you can take Jesus and share Him?

Week 3

Introduction: Why Is It Necessary to Have Witnesses?

Why is it necessary to have witnesses to anything? Witnesses create a believability to our story so that others will know that what we say is true. If I say I am five foot seven inches tall and I get measured by the doctor and he and two nurses are standing there seeing the same thing, then my statement has been confirmed. So why did Jesus deem it necessary to have witnesses to His resurrection? Jesus didn't want the lies of people saying that people stole his body to become the truth. He wants us to believe that He rose again because that's the truth. "We serve a Risen Savior and He's in the world today!" (Hymnal). There was a progression of people that witnessed Jesus after His resurrection, and they were from all walks of life. Why is this important? So that it would be corroborated with no bias. He talked with women, random men, a man that doubted, and His closest friends plus many more that we can research and discover on our own. The stories of these people are true and exciting. I mean, think about it, they just saw Jesus die an awful death on the cross. They watched people put Him in a tomb and watched them roll a stone in front of the tomb, and now three days later, Jesus rose again! That's hard to believe. But it doesn't make it any less true. Read the stories and be transported back in time and feel their excitement, their disbelief, and their acknowledgment of the truth, and then live out the fact that we too serve that same Risen Savior and "He's in our hearts today."

Day 1

Mary Magdalene

Mary Magdalene is the story of grace. So many sermons have been preached talking about how she was a prostitute and possibly even the woman that was caught in adultery and Jesus said, "Go and sin no more." But I haven't seen proof of either. But that's really not the point. The point is that she was not living for Jesus, and when she met Him, He changed her life completely. She became an avid follower of Jesus and was often found with the disciples serving alongside of Him. She loved Jesus with her whole heart and lived that change.

> Read John 20:1–18; Matthew 28:1–10; Mark 16:1–8; Luke 24:1–12.
>
> Now on the first day of the week Mary Magdalene came early to the tomb, while it was still dark, and saw the stone already taken away from the tomb. So she ran and came to Simon Peter and to the other disciple whom Jesus loved, and said to them, "They have taken away the Lord out of the tomb, and we do not know where they have laid Him." So, Peter and the other disciple went forth, and they were going to the tomb. The two were running together; and the other disciple ran ahead faster than Peter and came to

the tomb first; and stooping and looking in, he saw the linen wrappings lying there; but he did not go in. And so, Simon Peter also came, following him, and entered the tomb; and he saw the linen wrappings lying there, and the face-cloth which had been on His head, not lying with the linen wrappings, but rolled up in a place by itself. So the other disciple who had first come to the tomb then also entered, and he saw and believed. For as yet they did not understand the Scripture that He must rise again from the dead. So the disciples went away again to their own homes.

But Mary was standing outside the tomb weeping; and so, as she wept, she stooped and looked into the tomb and she saw two angels in white sitting, one at the head and one at the feet, where the body of Jesus had been lying. And they said to her, "Woman, why are you weeping?" She said to them, "Because they have taken away my Lord, and I do not know where they have laid Him." When she had said this, she turned around and saw Jesus standing there, and did not know that it was Jesus. Jesus said to her, "Woman, why are you weeping? Whom are you seeking?" Supposing Him to be the gardener, she said to Him, "Sir, if you have carried Him away, tell me where you have laid Him, and I will take Him away." Jesus said to her, "Mary!" She turned and said to Him in Hebrew, "Rabboni!" (which means, Teacher). Jesus said to her, "Stop clinging to Me, for I have not yet ascended to the Father; but go to My brethren and say to them, 'I ascend to My Father and your Father, and My God and your God.'" Mary Magdalene came, announcing to the disciples, "I have seen the Lord," and that He had said these things to her."

Now after the Sabbath, as it began to dawn toward the first day of the week, Mary Magdalene and the other Mary came to look at the grave. And behold, a severe earthquake had occurred, for an angel of the Lord descended from heaven and came and rolled away the stone and sat upon it. And his appearance was like lightning, and his clothing as white as snow. The guards shook for fear of him and became like dead men. The angel said to the women, "Do not be afraid; for I know that you are looking for Jesus who has been crucified. He is not here, for He has risen, just as He said. Come, see the place where He was lying. Go quickly and tell His disciples that He has risen from the dead; and behold, He is going ahead of you into Galilee, there you will see Him; behold, I have told you."

And they left the tomb quickly with fear and great joy and ran to report it to His disciples. And behold, Jesus met them and greeted them. And they came up and took hold of His feet and worshiped Him. Then Jesus said to them, "Do not be afraid; go and take word to My brethren to leave for Galilee, and there they will see Me."

When the Sabbath was over, Mary Magdalene, and Mary the mother of James, and Salome, bought spices, so that they might come and anoint Him. Very early on the first day of the week, they came to the tomb when the sun had risen. They were saying to one another, "Who will roll away the stone for us from the entrance of the tomb?" Looking up, they saw that the stone had been rolled away, although it was extremely large. Entering the tomb, they saw a young man sitting at the right, wearing a white robe; and they were amazed. And he said to them, "Do not be amazed; you are looking for Jesus the Nazarene, who has been crucified. He has risen; He is not here; behold, here is the place where they laid Him. "But go, tell His disciples and Peter, 'He is going ahead of you to Galilee; there you will see Him, just as He told you.'" They went out and fled from the tomb, for trembling and astonishment had gripped them; and they said nothing to anyone, for they were afraid.

But on the first day of the week, at early dawn, they came to the tomb bringing the spices which they had prepared. And they found the stone rolled away from the tomb, but when they entered, they did not find the body of the Lord Jesus. While they were perplexed about this, behold, two men suddenly stood near them in dazzling clothing; and as the women were terrified and bowed their faces to the ground, the men said to them, "Why do you seek the living One among the dead? He is not here, but He has risen. Remember how He spoke to you while He was still in Galilee, saying that the Son of Man must be delivered into the hands of sinful men, and be crucified, and the third day rise again." And they remembered His words, and returned from the tomb and reported all these things to the eleven and to all the rest. Now they were Mary Magdalene and Joanna and Mary the mother of James; also, the other women with them were telling these things to the apostles. But these words appeared to them as nonsense, and they would not believe them. But Peter got up and ran to the tomb; stooping and looking in, he saw the linen wrappings only; and he went away to his home, marveling at what had happened.

Notice from reading all four accounts of the same story, there are slight differences. Some stories are incredibly detailed, and some tell an overview account. Does that make one story less true than the others? No, it's just how that writer wanted to portray that portion of the story. If four people are eyewitnesses to a wreck, each person will have similar stories because it's the same wreck, but what they deem important in the account may differ slightly. One might focus on the victims, one might focus on the overall scene, one might focus on the rescuers, and one may focus on the crowd. All four were at the scene and saw the same thing, but the details will always be slightly different. It's the same with the gospels. Each of the writers focused on a different aspect on the account, but we do know that Mary Magdalene along with several other women went early in the morning on the third day to do the final burial rituals and they were the first to visit the tomb after the resurrection. Mary went and told the disciples and immediately returned to the tomb to get a full grasp on what happened.

This is my favorite part of the story. In John 20:11, you can see the complete devastation of Mary. The disciples came and saw the tomb was empty and went back to their homes. Mary, on the other hand, felt lost. Here Jesus, her Lord and Savior, was dead, *then* she discovers that He has disappeared, *and now* her hope is completely gone, and she has no one to turn to in her hour of need.

She looks in the tomb and sees two angels sitting where Jesus' body laid—one at the top and one at the bottom. They ask her why she's crying. If I were her, I would start being very sarcastic. I would've said, "Well, you are sitting where my Lord laid. He is gone and you are asking *me* why *I'm* crying?" But Mary simply said, "They've taken my Lord, and I don't know where to find him." I don't know if it was a niggling feeling of knowing someone was watching her or she heard something behind her but she turned around. A man was standing there, and He asked her the same question, "Woman, why are you crying?" She might've gotten tired of hearing that question because she said, "If you've taken him somewhere, please tell me so I can go get Him." She had no idea she was talking with Jesus, but as soon as He said her name in the voice that had become so precious to her, she knew. He looked at her and said, "Mary." One word and she knew. His voice for Mary was like a child hearing his/her parent's voice. There is a distinction to hearing a voice that we have heard all our life. We can pick out that voice in a crowd and know they are needing our help or just calling us for dinner but we know it well. Mary knew Jesus' voice, and she knew it well. When He called her name, her eyes were opened to the reality that her Lord was standing right in front of her. In Matthew 28:9, it said, "She clasped his feet and worshipped Him." Jesus had plans, and He knew Mary was perfect in gathering the disciples. He told her to go and tell the disciples to go to Galilee and He would meet them there. She was obedient to the tasks Jesus had called her to do, and she left Him at the tomb. I'm sure, though, she just wanted to stay in His presence, ask questions about how it all happened, but she was obedient.

Sometimes, we don't have all the answers, and many times, we just want to sit at Jesus' feet and study His Word because that's where the comfort lies. But Jesus tells us to go and gather others to Him, and our only answer should be, "Okay, I'll go." Mary knew that she would see Him again because He said He would see them in Galilee. Every day, we have a chance to sit and be in His presence. But after we have our strength from Him, we are to go and bring others to Him.

Worship at His feet today, then go out and bring others to Him. Jesus commands this of us all.

Day 2

The Men on the Emmaus Road

Read Luke 24:13–35.

"And behold, two of them were going that very day to a village named Emmaus, which was about seven miles from Jerusalem. And they were talking with each other about all these things which had taken place. While they were talking and discussing, Jesus Himself approached and began traveling with them. But their eyes were prevented from recognizing Him. And He said to them, "What are these words that you are exchanging with one another as you are walking?" And they stood still, looking sad. One of them, named Cleopas, answered and said to Him, "Are You the only one visiting Jerusalem and unaware of the things which have happened here in these days?" And He said to them, "What things?" And they said to Him, "The things about Jesus the Nazarene, who was a prophet mighty in deed and word in the sight of God and all the people, and how the chief priests and our rulers delivered Him to the sentence of death, and crucified Him. But we were hoping that it was He who was going to redeem Israel. Indeed, besides all this, it is the third day since these things happened. But also some women among us amazed us. When they were at the tomb early in the morning, and did not find His body, they came, saying that they had also seen a vision of angels who said that He was alive. Some of those who were with us went to the tomb and found it just exactly as the women also had said; but Him they did not see." And He said to them, "O foolish men and slow of heart to believe in all that the prophets have spoken! Was it not necessary for the Christ to suffer these things and to enter into His glory?" Then beginning with Moses and with all the prophets, He explained to them the things concerning Himself in all the Scriptures.

And they approached the village where they were going, and He acted as though He were going farther. But they urged Him, saying, "Stay with us, for it is getting toward evening, and the day is now nearly over." So He went in to stay with them. When He had reclined at the table with them, He took the bread and blessed it, and breaking it, He began giving it to them. Then their eyes were opened and they recognized Him; and He vanished from their sight. They said to one another, "Were not our hearts burning within us while He was speaking to us on the road, while He was explaining the Scriptures to us?" And they got up that very hour and returned to Jerusalem, and found gathered together the eleven and those who were with them, saying, "The Lord has really risen and has appeared to Simon." They began to relate their experiences on the road and how He was recognized by them in the breaking of the bread.

Oblivious. Jesus was right there! He was walking beside them as they walked the road to Emmaus. And what were they talking about? Jesus! The man walking beside them! They had no clue. They had no hope.

The disciples had just gone to see the empty tomb and came back and reported to the rest of them that the tomb was empty and no one knew where he was. They had heard that angels had told the women that Jesus was alive, but so far, no one had any proof. Until proof arrived, hopelessness remained. Yet as these two men walked down the road, Jesus shows up and begins walking with them. He asked them what they were discussing.

Question: Have you ever been some place where a big story breaks and that's all people talk about? Then someone new comes along and wants to join in on the conversation, but we have to fill them in to catch up to where you are in the story. Sometimes, it is a little frustrating because we feel like everyone should know what's going on since the story is so big. That is the feeling of the two men when Jesus asked them about their conversation.

Cleopas (one of the men) looked at Jesus with shock and basically said, "Are you kidding me? This story is the talk of the town! Jesus was crucified then buried, and now angels are telling our friends that he is alive! Have you not heard any of this? We are just processing it all as we walk to Emmaus because all of it is so hard to believe!" Jesus sort of reprimands them for being so slow to believe, and then He begins to explain the scripture starting with Moses and the prophets. Not only that, He ties Himself to every bit of scripture and how He had come to fulfill all of the scripture. Yet Jesus kept them from knowing who He really was.

I'm not really sure how long their journey was on the road to Emmaus, but Jesus Himself was with them the entire time! How many times do we go through our days and we have Jesus right beside us, guiding us, teaching us, showing us the way and we don't recognize Him? In the process, we begin to see what is wrong with the day and what's wrong around us and our focus goes from the One of hope to a focus of despair and hopelessness.

The three of them make it to Emmaus, and because it's late, they invite Him to stay with them. Jesus agrees. He takes the bread, gives thanks, breaks it, and gives it to them, and immediately their eyes are opened to what was right in front of them all along! And then He disappeared. "Jesus! He was right here! Why didn't we see that before now? Could we not sense that in our spirits? We were so focused on our own helplessness that we couldn't see what was right in front of us!" As soon as they realized, they got up and went right back to Jerusalem (where they had just come from). Can you imagine? They had just walked from Jerusalem to Emmaus, and now they were running straight back. What a journey for one day!

They had to tell the disciples. They were witnesses of the truth, and they couldn't contain their excitement. They said, "It is true! The Lord has risen and has appeared to Simon." Then they shared their entire experience all the way up to when he broke the bread and disappeared.

Question: Have you had a chance to walk with Jesus and not realize it was Him?

Every day, we have an opportunity to walk with Jesus, and every day, we have the ability to recognize Him at work around us or not. If we don't see Him working, we miss the blessing. If we do notice Him, we can really grow in His love and power and truly glorify Him in all that we do.

Jesus is walking with us today. Will today be the day that we realize that He has been there all along to bring us hope? We just have to acknowledge Him, believe in Him, and receive Him.

Jesus is walking with us today. Sing with Him. Love on Him. Give Him glory and honor and praise. He alone deserves it.

Day 3

The Disciples

Read John 20:1–9, 19–23.

Now on the first day of the week Mary Magdalene came early to the tomb, while it was still dark, and saw the stone already taken away from the tomb. So she ran and came to Simon Peter and to the other disciple whom Jesus loved, and said to them, "They have taken away the Lord out of the tomb, and we do not know where they have laid Him." So, Peter and the other disciple went forth, and they were going to the tomb. The two were running together; and the other disciple ran ahead faster than Peter and came to the tomb first; and stooping and looking in, he saw the linen wrappings lying there; but he did not go in. And so, Simon Peter also came, following him, and entered the tomb; and he saw the linen wrappings lying there, and the face-cloth which had been on His head, not lying with the linen wrappings, but rolled up in a place by itself. So the other disciple who had first come to the tomb then also entered, and he saw and

> believed. For as yet they did not understand the Scripture that He must rise again from the dead.
>
> So when it was evening on that day, the first day of the week, and when the doors were shut where the disciples were, for fear of the Jews, Jesus came and stood in their midst and said to them, "Peace be with you." And when He had said this, He showed them both His hands and His side. The disciples then rejoiced when they saw the Lord. So Jesus said to them again, "Peace be with you; as the Father has sent Me, I also send you." And when He had said this, He breathed on them and said to them, "Receive the Holy Spirit. If you forgive the sins of any, their sins have been forgiven them; if you retain the sins of any, they have been retained."

Depressed. Scared. Jumpy. Paranoid. These all could be words to describe the disciples after Jesus was crucified. They had a fear that if the people could kill Jesus, then all His followers were going to be next. So they remained behind locked doors all together. When Mary came to tell them about what they had seen, I'm sure all the emotions swirled around them at one time: disbelief, hope, excitement, and an adrenaline rush. Whatever we can think of, it probably swirled around in their minds. Mary had to convince them to open the door but had to run to keep up with them as soon as she told them. John was the first to get to the open tomb, but Peter went straight into the tomb to find only the cloths lying where Jesus had been. As soon as Peter went in, John followed and saw the linens separate from the face cloth and immediately believed.

The disciples eventually left, but Mary stayed and had the privilege of seeing Jesus first. She also got the privilege to be His messenger to the disciples twice. The second time, she came back with a message from Jesus to the disciples. He wanted to see them! In order to see Jesus, though, Mary told them they had to go to Galilee to a certain place. They didn't hesitate. If there was any chance that Jesus was alive, they were going to go. They could've sat back and waved Mary off by saying she was crazy, but they needed the hope to hold on to. They needed Jesus to be alive! The only way they could substantiate Mary's statements was to go where she told them.

They were still scared, though, because if we notice in verse 19, it says, "The disciples were together with the doors locked for fear of the Jews." They wanted to believe, but the fear of the people was still strong within them. The great thing is that Jesus didn't knock on the door and wait for them to let him in—He just appeared. He did this several more times with the disciples. Two of those times were with locked doors, which show that even though they had seen Jesus, they still were afraid of the Jews. They had received the Holy Spirit from Jesus in their first meeting, but the complete boldness came after Jesus ascended into heaven, and the Holy Spirit came down like rain on everyone.

I noticed that both times Jesus came into the locked rooms, He started with, "Peace be with you." Then He showed His hands and side. They too believed when they saw with their own eyes, but the doubt wasn't as prominent as the fear. Jesus set their minds at ease as to whether He was a ghost or real in Luke 24:36–49. He made them touch his flesh. He ate some fish in their presence and then began to teach them about how He had fulfilled the Law and the prophets. He opened their minds to completely understand what scriptures had said, "The Christ will suffer and rise from the dead on the third day and repentance and forgiveness of sins will be preached in his name to all nations beginning at Jerusalem." He then told them that they were witnesses of all these things but to stay in the city until the Father had clothed them with the power of the Holy Spirit.

The third time Jesus appeared to His disciples was by the Sea of Tiberias. Peter wanted to go fishing, so they all went out and caught nothing all night. Jesus appeared on the shore and yelled out to them, asking what they had caught. They said nothing, so Jesus said to cast their nets on the other side. Immediately, they had so many fish that the nets started to break, and they had to get help from another boat. John recognized Jesus and told Peter. Peter was so excited that he jumped out of the boat and swam to shore while the rest of them brought the boat in with all the fish. When they came into shore, Peter then helped, but he was so excited that the fish were insignificant to the fact that Jesus was with them again. Jesus had a fire with fish and bread ready for them to eat together.

Fear played a big factor in keeping them from being all that Jesus had for them at the time, but faith played a bigger part in spreading the gospel throughout the world.

Question: What plays a bigger part in your life, the fear of what others think or faith for an eternal future?

The disciples saw Jesus, they touched Jesus, they ate with Jesus, they believed in Jesus, then they told everyone about our Risen Savior.

Question: What do you say, fear or faith? Choose today.

Day 4

Thomas

Read John 20:24–29.

Now Thomas (also known as Didymus), one of the Twelve, was not with the disciples when Jesus came. So the other disciples told him, "We have seen the Lord!"

But he said to them, "Unless I see the nail marks in his hands and put my finger where the nails were, and put my hand into his side, I will not believe."

A week later, his disciples were in the house again, and Thomas was with them. Though the doors were locked, Jesus came and stood among them and said, "Peace be with you!" Then he said to Thomas, "Put your finger here; see my hands. Reach out your hand and put it into my side. Stop doubting and believe."

Thomas said to him, "My Lord and my God!"

Then Jesus told him, "Because you have seen me, you have believed; blessed are those who have not seen and yet have believed."

There are times in our lives where some events just seem to be too good to be true. And no matter how many people try to tell us it's true, we just won't believe it until we can see it for ourselves. Welcome to the life of Thomas.

For some reason, not told in the Bible, Thomas was not with the disciples when Mary came to tell them about Jesus' tomb being empty. He was not with them when they went to check out the tomb, and he wasn't with them when they were in Galilee when Jesus came into a locked room. So we can imagine his thoughts when the disciples ran up to him and said, "We have seen the Lord!" (v. 25). He said to them, "Unless I see the nail marks in his hands and put my finger when the nails were and put my hand in his side, I will not believe it." (v.26) Basically, he thought the disciples had gotten together and decided to play a practical joke on him since he hadn't been with them on those other occasions.

So, a week later, Thomas was with the disciples in another house with doors locked, and Jesus appeared and stood among them. He immediately spoke to put their hearts at rest by saying, "Peace be with you." The reason he did that probably was because he startled them by just appearing in a room that was locked yet again. Jesus looked at Thomas and knew of his unbelief. He didn't question why he didn't believe. He simply said, "Put your finger here; see my hands. Reach out and put your hand in my side. Stop doubting and believe" (v. 27). It doesn't say that he actually touched his sides or his hands, but after seeing Jesus, he cried out, "My Lord and My God!" Truth is revealed. Belief is made into reality.

Oh, if it were only that simple. Jesus did a simple reprimand of Thomas that is a reprimand to us all at different point in our life. He said, "Because you have seen me, you have believed. Blessed are those who believe who have not seen and yet have believed." Basically, the only way Thomas was going to believe the truth was if he saw Jesus for himself as a witness. He is not alone but really takes the brunt of doubting. In fact, if someone doubts something to be true, they are usually called a "Doubting Thomas."

Faith or lack of faith, that is the question. Matthew 17:20 says, "If you have faith as small as a mustard seed, you can say to this mountain, 'Move from here to there' and it will move. Nothing will be impossible for you." So why did Thomas think that Jesus couldn't have risen from the dead? He had been with this man for three solid years—watching Him heal the sick, the lame, the blind, the deaf, and the mute. He watched Jesus raise Lazarus from the dead and still lacked the faith to believe. But if you think about it, the other disciples had a hard time believing as well when Mary came and told them about the tomb. They ran to see it for themselves. When Mary told them to go to Galilee and Jesus would meet them there, I bet many of them went just to see if it were true. So even though Thomas expressed his disbelief out loud, many expressed their disbelief inwardly.

When Jesus said, "Blessed are those who believe who have not seen," that is anyone that has believed that Jesus died for our sins and rose again and is alive today. We didn't have the luxury to see Jesus in person, but that's where faith comes in. We believe that one day Jesus is coming back for His children and then our faith will be substantiated. Until that day, we trust that God's Word is true. We trust the witnesses that spent time with Jesus. We simply trust. We simply believe. And then live it out for all to see.

Day 5

Peter

When it comes to restoration and change, as well as being a witness of the Risen Savior, Peter always comes to my mind. I can relate to Peter on so many levels:

- The excitement of following Jesus and dropping everything to follow Him.
- The desire to accommodate everyone for Jesus.
- The audacity to say I'll do one thing when Jesus knows quite well that I will do the opposite.
- The desire to love and serve Him on one level when He asks for more, knowing full well I'm not ready spiritually and then accepts me when I am.
- When all is said and done, love Him unconditionally, and live for Him unabandoned and unashamed of the gospel.

Read John 21:15–23.

> When they had finished eating, Jesus said to Simon Peter, "Simon son of John, do you love me more than these?"
>
> "Yes, Lord," he said, "you know that I love you."
>
> Jesus said, "Feed my lambs."

> Again Jesus said, "Simon son of John, do you love me?"
>
> He answered, "Yes, Lord, you know that I love you."
>
> Jesus said, "Take care of my sheep."
>
> The third time he said to him, "Simon son of John, do you love me?"
>
> Peter was hurt because Jesus asked him the third time, "Do you love me?" He said, "Lord, you know all things; you know that I love you."
>
> Jesus said, "Feed my sheep. Very truly I tell you, when you were younger you dressed yourself and went where you wanted; but when you are old you will stretch out your hands, and someone else will dress you and lead you where you do not want to go." Jesus said this to indicate the kind of death by which Peter would glorify God. Then he said to him, "Follow me!"
>
> Peter turned and saw that the disciple whom Jesus loved was following them. (This was the one who had leaned back against Jesus at the supper and had said, "Lord, who is going to betray you?") When Peter saw him, he asked, "Lord, what about him?"
>
> Jesus answered, "If I want him to remain alive until I return, what is that to you? You must follow me." Because of this, the rumor spread among the believers that this disciple would not die. But Jesus did not say that he would not die; he only said, "If I want him to remain alive until I return, what is that to you?"

In the Greek language, there are several different words to say love.

Agape means unconditional love. It is a love that is given freely and fully without need for anything in return. It is a love that only

God can offer to His children and our job is to receive. We, as humans, have trouble giving love without expecting something in return so many people have a hard time receiving Jesus into their hearts because they can't imagine anyone doing that for them.

Phileo means brotherly love. This is a love that humans have toward each other. Philadelphia is called the city of brotherly love because its name is taken from that Greek word. This love allows us to have that friendship and connection with someone else. As a brother/sister, we would protect and support them in any way possible.

Eros means an intimate love with is typically found in a marriage relationship between a man and a woman.

Peter has dealt with quite a bit over the last couple of days and weeks, and he is emotionally spent. Before Jesus was crucified, Jesus predicted that Peter would deny Him three times before the rooster crowed (Matthew 26:31–35). And sure enough, in Matthew 26:31, it said, "The sheep are scattered," and now Peter is on his own and not so tough. A peasant girl asked him if he was one of the ones with Jesus and without his support, he denied Jesus strongly three times, and then the rooster crowed. He was devastated. He needed restoration. He needed forgiveness. He needed grace. But Jesus was dead, and then He wasn't! A second chance! A time to start over! Time to make things right!

After Jesus had resurrected, he met the disciples at the water. The men came in from fishing, and everyone ate the fish they had caught. Jesus pulled Peter aside and began to question his level of love for Jesus in John 21:15–23. Peter was eager to love Jesus. But Peter's ability to love at the level that Jesus was asking for just wasn't there. John 21:15–17 reads a little differently when you insert the Greek words of love to replace the English word for love. It reads like this: "Simon, son of John, do you *agape* me (love me unconditionally) more than these?" Peter said, "Yes, Lord, you know I *phileo* you (love you like a brother)." Jesus said, "Feed my lambs." Again, Jesus said, "Simon, son of John, do you *agape* me?" Peter said, "Yes, Lord, you know I phileo you."

"Take care of my sheep." The third time, Jesus asked, "Simon, son of John, do you *phileo* me?"

Saddened because he asked a third time, "Lord, you know all things, you know I *phileo* you."

"Feed my sheep."

Jesus wanted Peter to love him unconditionally, but all Peter could do at the moment was love Jesus like a brother. Jesus understood and accepted him where he was. Jesus needed Peter to understand the level of love that he had for Jesus so he knew where he was and where he needed to be. The beautiful thing is, even though it began at phileo after his restoration, he ended with agape by dying on the cross upside down because of his love for Jesus.

If we read through the book of Acts, we will see that Peter was a pivotal part of starting the early church. He was no longer ashamed of saying that he walked with Jesus, learned from Jesus, and was a witness of His resurrection. He was completely changed, and the Spirit of the Lord made Him bold in His witness. At the end of his ministry, they ordered him to be crucified, but he didn't feel worthy to be crucified the same way, so he was crucified upside down. His phileo love had been transformed into agape love.

Question: How deep is your love for God? How can you love and serve Him today?

His love spans wider than the skies and deeper than the oceans. He died for us and is coming back for us. He longs to hear from us and be loved by us. He loves us very much.

Week 4

Introduction: Why Do We Call Life a Journey?

Why do we call life a journey? Why not stop when we get tired? Why not say a prayer of belief and then be done and live as we want knowing that we are safe from hell? It's simple really—life is all about the journey. As the old hymn says, "This earth is not my home, I'm just a passin' through." Well, if it's true that we are just passing through, then we have to be moving in some form or fashion. Passing through requires movement, not being stationary. Stationary allows you to go nowhere. So once we become a Christian, our journey changes. Our destination changes. Everything about us changes. Will it be a difficult journey? Yes. Look at Jesus. His life was not roses and chocolate. It was brutal at times but necessary to complete the journey that he began. Will we have great days? Absolutely. And it's those days that are landmarks of growth to help us over our next hurdle. I love the book called *The Pilgrim's Progress* or *Hind's Feet on High Places* because it is a story about the journey that all Christians must walk. It's challenging, convicting, but rewarding in the long run. Jesus came so we have a complete example to follow in our everyday lives. God knew we needed to see God in skin form, but He also knew we needed a Savior, so He gave us both in Jesus. It's time to get ready for the journey. Our destination awaits.

Day 1

Planning

(Choosing the Right Direction)

So we are beginning our journey! Yay! I love maps. They show me where I want to go, how to get there, and if there are several routes to get to the same place. I sometimes wish I were a bird because a straight line between two points is always the shortest distance. However, since I don't have wings, I have to take a car on most trips. Some journeys are curvy, hilly, and some just seem like I have to go out of my way just to get to where I want to go. But in all cases, I have to choose the right direction, and that takes planning.

The Christian journey is the same way. We have to know the right direction to go and plan accordingly or our trip could be stopped before it gets started. So for the Christian journey, it begins with knowing the plan of salvation. Romans 3:23 says, "For all have sinned and fall short of the glory of God." It doesn't say some or a few; it says *all* have sinned. That means all of us. If a gap between two ledges is fifty feet and you say you can jump thirty-five feet and I say I can jump forty feet, we both still fall short of the fifty feet, and we both will still die. That's the bad news. The good news is coming.

Romans 6:23 says, "For the wages of sin is death but the gift of God is eternal life in Christ Jesus our Lord." We cannot earn our way into heaven. We can't be good enough to finally ask Jesus into our heart because as we just discovered we all fall short. Instead, Jesus gave us a gift, free of charge, no work required. The only thing we have to do is to take it. When kids get their presents at Christmas, they don't say, "What do I have to do to make this mine?" Nope, they eagerly grab it. Most times, they say thank you, rip it open, and run off to play with whatever it is. Adults, on the other hand, are skeptical and don't as readily take gifts offered to them. Why? Because they have been hardened by the world and have had their trust broken time after time. That is why Jesus said that we need to come to Jesus as a little child because they aren't hardened and offer themselves fully to what they receive.

Romans 10:9–10 says, "If you confess with your mouth, Jesus is Lord and believe in your heart that God raised him from the dead, you will be saved. For it is with your heart that you believe and are justified and it is with your mouth that you confess and are saved." Two things we need to do when receiving this free gift of salvation is confessing Jesus as Lord with our mouth so that everyone knows who we are now, including Satan, and then believe what we are saying in our heart. Don't just offer up lip service to Jesus because all we would be doing is putting on a show for everyone and Jesus doesn't want a show by an actor/actress; He wants all of us. If we do these two things, salvation is ours.

Romans 10:13 says, "Everyone who calls on the name of the Lord will be saved." Excuses for not calling on the name of the Lord are but not limited to:

- "I'm not worthy." Correct! No one is except for Jesus Himself.
- "I'm good enough." No one is good, not one except for Jesus Himself.
- "I haven't done many bad things like some people." Lying is breaking one of the Ten Commandments. Even if you thought about it, that's another commandment broken. Remember in Romans 3:23, it says, "*All* have sinned." Not doing bad things doesn't get you into heaven.

- "You should see my friend or family member. They claim to be Christian, but they are far from it! If that's what Christianity is like I don't want any part of it." Everyone will have to stand up for their own lives. We can only answer for our life. If at the end of our life Jesus says to us, "Why should I let you into my heaven?" and we say, "I am better than whoever," but never ask Jesus into our heart, He will say, "Depart from me, I never knew you!" There are no excuses in heaven. We either have Jesus in our heart or we don't. The only way to heaven is through Jesus.

John 3:16 says, "For God so loved the world that He gave His one and only Son, that *whosoever* believes in Him will not perish but have eternal life." Whosoever means you. Whosoever means me. Whosoever means whosoever. There are two deaths for sinners *not* saved by grace—the physical death and the death that leads us to hell (the spiritual death). God promises that because He sent His son to die in our place for our sins when He didn't have to that if we believe in Him, we will not die the second death instead we will live in heaven with Him.

Now that we know how to read our map, tomorrow, we will talk about how to pack for our journey. What will we pack for? Heaven? Hell? There are only two choices. Choose the wise path.

Day 2

Packing

What to pack? What to pack? That is always the question that plagues my mind for days before we go on vacation. I have to know where we are going, how many days will we be gone, what the weather is going to be like. Will we have a washer and dryer? What activities are we planning on doing? And the questions continue until we actually drive out of the driveway because until that moment, I still have access to things to bring. Once I am in a moving car, we do not turn back. If I have forgotten something, then we just either go without or buy it when we get there. Same with our Christian journey, questions on what to pack will plague us until we actually commit to the journey and begin moving forward. So let's start packing. God's ultimate desire is that we all pack for heaven. In order to know what to pack, let's start with what not to pack.

> Read Galatians 5:19–21.
>
> Now the deeds of the flesh are evident, which are: immorality, impurity, sensuality, idolatry, sorcery, enmities, strife, jealousy, outbursts of anger, disputes, dissensions, factions, envying, drunkenness, carousing, and things like these, of which I forewarn you, just as I have forewarned

> you, that those who practice such things will not inherit the kingdom of God.

In Galatians 5, Paul listed what was of the flesh which is of this world, and it is an easy trap to get into. But with most traps, they don't start out looking dangerous; instead, they look very enticing and inviting. Don't be fooled by the pretty wrappings that are full of nothing but deceit. Paul said that if we "pack" sexual immorality, moral impurity, promiscuity, idolatry (anything we consider more important than God), sorcery, hatred, strife, jealousy, anger, selfish ambition, dissension, envy, drunkenness, and anything similar to that, we will not inherit the kingdom of God. Since this world makes it amazingly simple and convenient to access whatever we desire at the click of a button, it is easy to lose focus and forget Who we are living for. So in packing for heaven, leave all that out of your luggage. There is so much more that we shouldn't pack, but I truly want to focus on what to pack so we can get going.

Read Ephesians 4:22–24; Galatians 5:22–23.

> That, in reference to your former manner of life, you lay aside the old self, which is being corrupted in accordance with the lusts of deceit, and that you be renewed in the spirit of your mind, and put on the new self, which in the likeness of God has been created in righteousness and holiness of the truth.
>
> But the fruit of the Spirit is love, joy, peace, patience, kindness, goodness, faithfulness, gentleness, self-control; against such things there is no law.

Taking off the old self and putting on the new self, what does that mean? When I lost 110 pounds back in the day, I didn't continue to wear the same clothes from the beginning of my weight loss journey at the end because of two important factors. The first factor was that the old clothes didn't fit the new me. The clothes kept falling off. In fact, I kept one pair of pants so I could look back at how far I had come. So, when I took them out, I got my whole self in one leg of the pants, and my oldest son got in the other leg of the pants. I had come a long way. The second factor was I had completely changed on the inside as well. My thoughts were different. My attitude was different. My focus and determination were different. I was different. So as I "packed" for my day, I packed differently. Instead of putting my selfish desires of what I wanted, I put on thoughts and desires of what God wanted. "Love, joy, peace, patience, kindness, goodness, faithfulness, gentleness and self-control" (Galatians 5:22–23) became my focus. I was free from the old selfish me, and I had become brand new in my desires for Christ.

Read Ephesians 6:10–18.

> Finally, be strong in the Lord and in his mighty power. Put on the full armor of God, so that you can take your stand against the devil's schemes. For our struggle is not against flesh and blood, but against the rulers, against the authorities, against the powers of this dark world and against the spiritual forces of evil in the heavenly realms. Therefore put on the full armor of God, so that when the day of evil comes, you may be able to stand your ground, and after you have done everything, to stand. Stand firm then, with the belt of truth buckled around your waist, with the breastplate of righteousness in place, and with your feet fitted with the readiness that comes from the gospel of peace. In addition to all this, take up the shield of faith, with which you can extinguish all the flaming arrows of the evil one. Take the helmet of salvation and the sword of the Spirit, which is the word of God.

> And pray in the Spirit on all occasions with all kinds of prayers and requests. With this in mind, be alert and always keep on praying for all the Lord's people.

Besides the fruit of the Spirit, which should always remain fresh and full of life, the armor of God is very important for our luggage. The reason is without it, we are powerless to fight against the devil's schemes. With the armor, we have the power of God, and we can face anything that comes our way. When we are packing for this journey, just know that we have to be ready for anything because we are fighting against a cunning, manipulative, and skilled opponent. Lucky for us, if we are packing for heaven, we have the greatest warrior *ever* fighting on our behalf, and in the end, we already know He has the victory! So, with this precious armor, we are able to stand firm and be fearless.

The armor of God and the reasoning behind them is as follows:

1. *Belt of Truth*—Truth must be the foundation for our life without truth we have nothing.
2. *Breastplate of Righteousness*—Live a right life (protect our heart and lungs).
3. *Feet fitted with the Gospel of Peace*—Share the gospel with everyone we meet.
4. *Shield of Faith*—Fiery arrows of Satan will fly; our faith keeps us standing strong.
5. *Helmet of Salvation*—We must believe in our mind and heart that Jesus died for us then we can be saved.
6. *Sword of the Spirit—Word of God*—Study His Word daily so we can fight the battles that come our way.
7. Pray in the Spirit in all occasions—Whatever comes our way, we always have the Spirit of God with us.

That's a lot of luggage, but it's a long journey. The great thing about it all is that it is not burdensome but a joy and a pleasure to live a life for Christ. So let's get packed, and let the journey begin!

Day 3

The Journey

We are on our way! Our bags are in the car, the GPS is on, the car is in drive, and we are off! Now what? Do we just enjoy the ride and do nothing until our final destination? Not likely. When I am driving, if my eyes go off to the right, my car tends to go off to the right. If my eyes go to the left, so does my car. (Not always, just trying to make a point.) We have to stay focused on what lies before us. We have to look out for crazy drivers, deer that want to cross the road without looking both ways, children playing too close to the road, sleepiness that sets in, etc. The list is long for things that distract us. This is the same in the Christian journey.

Read 1 Peter 5:8–10.

> Be alert and of sober mind. Your enemy the devil prowls around like a roaring lion looking for someone to devour. Resist him, standing firm in the faith, because you know that the family of believers throughout the world is undergoing the same kind of sufferings.
>
> And the God of all grace, who called you to his eternal glory in Christ, after you have suffered a little while, will himself restore you and make you strong, firm and steadfast.

"Satan prowls around like a roaring lion waiting to devour you." Have you ever watched a lion sneak up on its prey? He is stealthy and amazingly quiet until it's too late. By the time the prey sees the lion, the prey only has time to think, "Uh-oh!" then he is eaten. But if we stay self-controlled (which is one of the fruit of the Spirit we packed) and resist him by standing firm in our faith, God Himself will keep us strong. This battle against Satan is not something we can do on our own. We must have Jesus to fight alongside us and for us.

Read Philippians 3:12–21.

> Not that I have already obtained all this, or have already arrived at my goal, but I press on to take hold of that for which Christ Jesus took hold of me. Brothers and sisters, I do not consider myself yet to have taken hold of it. But one thing I do: Forgetting what is behind and straining toward what is ahead, I press on toward the goal to win the prize for which God has called me heavenward in Christ Jesus.
>
> All of us, then, who are mature should take such a view of things. And if on some point you think differently, that too God will make clear to you. Only let us live up to what we have already attained.
>
> Join together in following my example, brothers and sisters, and just as you have us as a model, keep your eyes on those who live as we do. For, as I have often told you before and now tell you again even with tears, many live as enemies of the cross of Christ. Their destiny is destruction, their god is their stomach, and their glory is in their shame. Their mind is set on earthly things. But our citizenship is in heaven. And we eagerly await a Savior from there, the Lord Jesus Christ, who, by the power that enables him to

> bring everything under his control, will transform our lowly bodies so that they will be like his glorious body.

"Forgetting what is behind and straining for what is ahead, I press on toward the goal to win the prize for which God has called me heavenward in Christ Jesus" (3:14). We all have a rearview mirror in our car, and it is very helpful when we have to parallel park or back out of parking spaces. However, we can't drive a car by keeping our eyes focused on the rearview mirror or the past. If we do, then we might miss something amazing in front of us, or we might wreck because we didn't see the hazards ahead. Satan wants us to stay glued to the rearview mirror because it is yet another distraction from staying focused on our goal. We must press forward. When my youngest son, Eric, ran cross country, he just ran his race. He was focused at the starting line, and when the gun went off, his focus became the finish line. Cross-Country running is not easy. The course is hilly and rocky and sometimes narrow and curvy, but he knew he couldn't quit because he would eventually see the finish line. It's amazing, though, if one veers off the course, several others will follow because they either don't know the course or they are just so focused on running that they don't pay attention to where they are. We must stay focused on our journey with Christ. He will lead us in the right direction every time.

In Psalm 37:5–6, it says, "Commit your way to the Lord, trust in Him and He will do this: He will make your righteousness shine like the dawn, the justice of your cause like the noonday sun." When we commit to the Lord, our life changes. Our path of life changes. We change. He desires for us to be changed for good.

Read Colossians 1:10–14.

> So that you may live a life worthy of the Lord and please him in every way: bearing fruit in every good work, growing in the knowledge of God, being strengthened with all power accord-

> ing to his glorious might so that you may have great endurance and patience, and giving joyful thanks to the Father, who has qualified you to share in the inheritance of his holy people in the kingdom of light. For he has rescued us from the dominion of darkness and brought us into the kingdom of the Son he loves, in whom we have redemption, the forgiveness of sins.

Paul gives us a list of things that he prays over our life. These are all things that will carry us until we see Jesus:

- Live a life worthy of the Lord.
- Please Him in every way.
- Bear fruit in every good work (we packed these).
- Be strengthened in His power.
- Have great endurance and patience, and joyfully give thanks to the Father.
- Share in the inheritance of the saints in the kingdom.
- Know that we have been saved from the darkness (which is the grip of Satan's hand) to full redemption and forgiveness in Christ.

Too much pressure? Can't do this journey on our own? Correct! This is not a journey taken alone. When Jesus is in our heart, the Holy Spirit becomes our companion, and He drives our car. We have to trust in where He is taking us and know that heaven is our destination.

I want to leave today with this scripture as just one more bit of cheerleading along our journey.

> And this is my prayer: that your love may abound more and more in knowledge and depth of insight so that you may be able to discern what is best and may be pure and blameless until the day of Christ filled with the fruit of righteousness

> that comes through Jesus Christ—to the glory and the praise of God. (Philippians 1:9–11)

Tired? Tomorrow, we rest in Jesus. Don't give up! Our destination is coming!

Day 4

Rest for the Journey

Read Genesis 2:1–2, Psalm 23:2–3a, and Matthew 11:28–30.

> Thus, the heavens and the earth were completed, and all their hosts. By the seventh day God completed His work which He had done, and He rested on the seventh day from all His work which He had done.
>
> "He makes me lie down in green pastures, He leads me beside quiet waters, He refreshes my soul.
>
> Come to me, all you who are weary and burdened, and I will give you rest. Take my yoke upon you and learn from me, for I am gentle and humble in heart, and you will find rest for your souls. For my yoke is easy and my burden is light.

Stress in the journey of life comes more often than we want to recognize it, and sometimes when it hits, it hits hard. During those times, our focus drifts from the path and calling that God has placed before us. The problems become bigger than the One that has the solution. Is that normal? Absolutely. In Genesis 1–2:2, God set the very first example of how to work and how to rest as well. He worked for six days and created the entire world, then on the seventh day, He rested. Why? Was He tired? No, God doesn't sleep or get weary. He did it for us to have an example to follow. He doesn't want us to be workaholics, but He doesn't want us to be lazy either. He wants us to work and, through our work, give Him the ultimate glory then take a day off to rest and enjoy the fruits of our labor. If we work constantly and don't stop to "smell the roses," what good is the work? Success comes from the enjoyment of the work.

I love what Psalm 23:2 says, "He *makes* me lie down in green pastures." That means many times I am so focused on my work that I lose sight of rest and I don't want to stop for even a day. I recall going back to work at the end of July to get ready for school to begin and I was asked the normal question, "How was your summer?" Instead of saying it was great and leave it at that, I began to breakdown Psalm 23 as my response. I told him that when we left for summer break, God made me rest for ten days at the beach, and He led me beside the quiet waters to help me to think and write. He restored my soul and rejuvenated my spirit so that I could come back into the Valley of the Shadow of Death. And I knew that God would be with me to walk me through it. I do not consider my job the Valley of the Shadow of Death because I love what I do but I was trying to make the point that I rested in His Spirit, I was revived, and now it was time to work. No matter what comes my way, I know that God has given me the strength to handle it.

Matthew 11:28–30 is a beautiful picture of ultimate care during stressful times. Are we burdened by something? Sickness? Work? Family? The list could go on forever. Are we weary? Too much weighing on our shoulders? We have a way out! Jesus wants to take it all and put it on His shoulders and give us His burden instead. The burden He wants to give us is lighter, more manageable, filled with joy and care. He wants to take our stress, worry, burdens, concerns, etc. and give us love, joy, peace, patience, kindness, goodness, gentleness, faithfulness, and self-control. Having those fruit of the Spirit brings about a different attitude in all situations to the point we can step back from the situation and look at it from a different perspective. When we rest in Jesus, it allows us to breathe easier, to think clearly, to laugh again, and to know that God's plan is perfect. In 2 Corinthians 12:9–10, it says, "My grace is sufficient for you, for my power is made perfect in weakness. Therefore, I will boast all the more gladly about my weaknesses so that Christ's power may rest on me. That is why for Christ's sake, I delight in weaknesses, in insults, in hardships, in persecutions, in difficulties. For when I am weak then I am strong."

So how do we finish our journey strong? By resting in God along with way. Let Him give us the strength to face difficult days so that the weight of it all doesn't seem so heavy and burdensome. Rest well so we can finish well. Only one more day!

Day 5

The Final Destination

Well, we made it to our final destination. What did we pack for? Heaven or hell? Still not decided? If that's our case, we are playing a dangerous game of Russian roulette because "no man/woman knows when his hour will come: as fish are caught in a net, or birds are caught in a snare, so men are trapped by evil times that fall unexpectantly upon them" (Ecclesiastes 9:12). And if we die while we are still deciding, God will decide for us. It says in Revelation 3:15–16, "I know your deeds, that you are neither cold nor hot. I wish you were either one or the other! So because you are lukewarm, neither hot nor cold—I am about to spit you out of my mouth," which means God will choose hell for us. I don't want that to happen to us. He is standing at the door of our heart knocking so we will open it and let Him in. As soon as we open that door, He will come in, and He is ours, and we are His (Revelation 3:20).

Read Revelation 20:11–15.

> Then I saw a great white throne and him who was seated on it. The earth and the heavens fled from his presence, and there was no place for them. And I saw the dead, great and small, standing before the throne, and books were opened. Another book was opened, which is the book

> of life. The dead were judged according to what they had done as recorded in the books. The sea gave up the dead that were in it, and death and Hades gave up the dead that were in them, and each person was judged according to what they had done. Then death and Hades were thrown into the lake of fire. The lake of fire is the second death. Anyone whose name was not found written in the book of life was thrown into the lake of fire.

At the end of time, every one of us will stand before God's throne to give an account for our lives. Justice says that we all deserve hell, but grace and mercy have given us a "golden ticket" to enter into God's heaven as His adopted sons and daughters. So at the Last Judgment, we will stand before God as individuals, based on our own decisions, not anyone else's for us, and God will say, "Why should I let you into my heaven?" If we say, "Because I was a good person or I wasn't like that person that *claimed* to know You or I didn't smoke or drink or have an adulterous affair or anything like that," then God will blatantly and sadly say, "Depart from Me, I never knew you" (Matthew 7:23). He will look in His Book of Life, and if our name isn't written in His book, then "you will be thrown into the lake of fire which is the second death" (Revelation 20:14–15).

But there is fantastic news for those that have received Jesus into their heart and if we have traveled on this journey and packed for heaven. When we stand before God and He says, "Why should I let you into My heaven?" We can proudly and boldly say, "I was bought with the blood of Jesus, and He lives in my heart today." Jesus will come along beside us as our attorney and say, "Dad, she's (he's) mine." God will smile down at us and say, "Well done, good and faithful servant! Welcome into your Father's kingdom! Come and share in your Master's happiness!" (Matthew 25:21).

When we walk into God's kingdom, it will be a truly breathtaking sight. The streets will be made of gold; the gate to walk through will be one giant pearl. It will shine with all the jewels of this world, but the purity of the gems will be so pure that God's light will shine brightly through it.

Read Revelation 21:1–7.

> Then I saw "a new heaven and a new earth," for the first heaven and the first earth had passed away, and there was no longer any sea. I saw the Holy City, the new Jerusalem, coming down out of heaven from God, prepared as a bride beautifully dressed for her husband. And I heard a loud voice from the throne saying, "Look! God's dwelling place is now among the people, and he will dwell with them. They will be his people, and God himself will be with them and be their God. 'He will wipe every tear from their eyes. There will be no more death' or mourning or crying or pain, for the old order of things has passed away."
>
> He who was seated on the throne said, "I am making everything new!" Then he said, "Write this down, for these words are trustworthy and true."
>
> He said to me: "It is done. I am the Alpha and the Omega, the Beginning and the End. To the thirsty I will give water without cost from the spring of the water of life. Those who are victorious will inherit all this, and I will be their God and they will be my children."

In heaven, there will be no more tears or sorrow or sin. Love, joy, and peace will reign over all. At the end of time, God will have destroyed this old earth, and He will bring down His new heaven and His new earth for us to live on for eternity, and Jesus will rule and reign over it all. Satan will be no more. What a glorious day that will be!

> Goodness and mercy will follow us all the days of our "new" lives and we will dwell in the house of the Lord forever. (Psalm 23:6)

Now doesn't that sound better than being thrown into the lake of fire to die a second time? So what are we waiting for? Today could be our last day, or we could have fifty years left to live. Either way, "Choose this day whom you will serve, but as for me and my family, we choose to serve the Lord" (Joshua 24:15). Come join us!

If you need to pray to ask Jesus in your heart, it is quite simple. Dear God, I believe that you sent your Son, Jesus, to Earth to die for my sins, then He rose three days later and coming back for me one day. Come into my heart today, and be Lord and Savior of my life. I love you!

If you prayed that today and you believe it, you are His from now through eternity. Go share that joy with someone (me, especially! I want to know so I can rejoice with you!).

It's been a pleasure pursuing Jesus with you this month. Continue your journey, and share Jesus with everyone you meet.

Once You PURSUE, You Must ***OBEY***

Book Two

This photo by Ann L. Knopp is licensed under CC BY.

Table of Contents

OBEY

Once You PURSUE, You Must OBEY

> *Does the Lord delight in burnt offerings and sacrifices as much as in obeying the LORD? To obey is better than sacrifice, and to heed (listen, pay attention) is better than the fat of rams.*
>
> —1 Samuel 15:22b

We have studied about pursuing Jesus with all of who we are, but there's more! It's not enough to discover our purpose and understand our calling; it all comes down to your own personal journey. Once we discover and understand, then what? We must obey! God said obedience is heads above the rest more important than the sacrifices of the day because obedience sacrifices ourselves. "Deny yourself and follow Jesus." That's what He wants. That's what He desires of each and every one of us. We'll study about those that obeyed God with their whole lives. We'll read about the ones that made the decision not to obey and what happened to them, and we will study the evidence of being obedient. But ultimately, it comes down to a personal decision in our own lives. Will we be obedient or not? What does it look like?

Follow me on this four-week-long journey into obedience, and then choose to follow and obey.

Introduction

God's timing is perfect. Therefore, He places the right people in the right places at the right time for His glory to shine brightest. The question comes: do we obey what He has set before us, or do we walk away? To obey or not to obey, that is the question for the next four weeks. We will see people that fully believed and obeyed and God did amazing things through them. Then we will see people that had the opportunity to obey but decided to walk away, leaving destruction in the wake.

Ultimately, decisions will make you or break you. God has plans for you, and if you choose to follow them, then you will find ultimate fulfillment as well as God will be glorified through you. Each day is filled with blessings that God wants/desires to bestow on you; however, He is not a needy God. He has the ability to do everything Himself with the help of no one, but He desires to include His own. To obey is to be included in the blessing. To say no means you miss out and He will use someone else. If He has chosen you, then it's time to listen and obey.

Section 1: Obedient Believers

Day 1

Noah: God Saves Those Who Obey

Noah was a righteous man, blameless among the people of his time, and he walked with God.
—Genesis 6:9

Noah was nine generations removed from Adam. That may not seem that long in the age of people today, but if you think about how long people lived back then, it turns into centuries of time.

Adam lived 930 years.
Enosh lived 905 years.
Mahalaliel lived 895 years.
Enoch lived 365 years, and then God took him away.
Methuselah lived 969 years.
And then came Noah.
Seth lived 912 years.
Jared lived 962 years.
Kenan lived 910 years.
Lamech lived 777 years.

So to say Noah didn't have children until he was five hundred years old seems young for that time. However, I can't even fathom being pregnant at that age. My bones creak at forty-nine. During all these long years of the past generations, people grew in number at a vast rate. Sin overtook everything, and the Lord grieved his decision of making man in the first place. The first thing God did was shorten the number of days people lived to 120 years. Then He decided to wipe the earth clean with the exception of Noah. "Noah found favor in the eyes of the Lord" (Genesis 6:8).

"The Lord doesn't look at the things people look at. People look at the outward appearance, but the Lord looks at the heart" (1 Samuel 16:7). This verse could've been reiterated throughout the Bible, and it certainly can be said today. We are so quick to judge others by their outward appearance that we forget about the soul and trying to bring others to Christ.

Noah preached and tried to bring others to God for one hundred years while he built the ark. "Noah was a righteous man, blameless among the people of his time, and he walked with God… Now the earth was corrupt in God's sight and was full of violence" (Genesis 6:9, 11). We think it's hard now to share Jesus with others, but imagine being the only one in the corrupt world that walked with God. We can only share so much of our heart, and Scripture can be shared daily, but until the Holy Spirit convicts the listener to hear what is being said, it falls on deaf ears.

God knew that Noah was going to preach to deaf ears but Noah continued to be obedient to the calling that God placed on his life. He had a task, and that was to build an ark that would be large enough for two of every creature in the world plus every kind of food and stored it to be eaten later by them throughout the flood and a place for his family to live.

I've been to see the Ark in Kentucky, and it is massive, but one thing I noticed was that every place was taken by something. It was designed to be filled with exactly who came to live on the ark. No more, no less. God knew the hearts of the people, and He knew they wouldn't get on the ark because to them it was a ridiculous notion to get on a boat in the middle of the desert that had never seen rain.

Yet Noah and his family were obedient. The animals were obedient to come. And all those that came were saved. It really is that simple. If you come to Jesus, you will be saved. If you don't, then life after death will not be a pleasant one for you. I don't want to see that for anyone. Noah preached for one hundred years while building the ark to save them from impending doom, but in the end, it was the ones that said "Yes" that were saved. If you haven't said "Yes" yet to Jesus, what are you waiting for? The end is coming. Which side of the ark door will you be on?

Day 2

Nehemiah

If you are unfaithful, I will scatter you among the nations, but if you return to me and obey my commands, then even if your exiled people are at the farthest horizon, I will gather them from there to the place I have chosen as a dwelling place for My name.

—Nehemiah 1:8–9

These words were quoted by Nehemiah but said by Moses back in Exodus, and Nehemiah believed in the power of the Lord. God saw his willingness to obey and gave him the power, determination, and means to complete his task. What was his task? To rebuild the wall of Jerusalem. Who was Nehemiah? "He was the cupbearer to the king" (1:11). He was a servant. He tasted the king's drink before the king so that if it was poisoned, the cupbearer would die in the king's place. Then if he did, then a new cupbearer would come in his place. He was replaceable. He was dispensable. Or was he? God saw Nehemiah as a leader. He saw him as a visionary. He saw him as bold. He saw him as fearless. And because God saw him in that light, the king held him in higher regard. He took notice of Nehemiah when he was troubled. He listened to Nehemiah when he was troubled. He listened to Nehemiah as he explained his concerns and how he wanted to help and what he needed to be able to build the walls of

Jerusalem. The king asked how long he would be gone, and that's all he needed to continue boldly. He asked for letters to various governors so he would be safe in his travels. He asked for a letter to receive wood from the king's woods for supplies, and everything was granted. Everything. Why? Because Nehemiah was being obedient to what God would have him do.

When he got to Jerusalem, he laid out his plan for the people, and each family got to work on a different section of the wall until the entire wall including the city gate were completed in fifty-two days. Fifty-two days! That's what I call working as a team.

Opposition came from Sanballot and his men, and Nehemiah had to regroup where half had to work while the others stood guard. Then Sanballot threatened to tell the king that Nehemiah was building a fortress so that he could become king which Nehemiah denied.

Throughout the entire building, despite the troubles, Nehemiah was obedient. He was faithful. He was focused. He was true to his word. He did what God called him to do. Because of that, the Jerusalem wall that was in ruins stood once again. The people that were vulnerable to attack were protected once again.

God does the same for us. He gives us a vision of what He wants done, and when He does that, He gives us the boldness, determination, focus, and means to complete what He has designed. God will always provide for His vision for the tasks He sets before us. We just have to be willing to be obedient in the process. When we are obedient, then we will see that only He is the one that can complete it in us. Our job is to be obedient. What has God shown you to start doing? Go boldly in His name today!

Day 3

Esther: Obedience Despite the Circumstances

And who knows but that you have come to this position for such a time as this?

—Esther 4:14b

I will continue to harp on two things whenever I write because I believe they resonate through the Bible in every story and in every life. One, I believe that every day we have a choice. We can choose to be obedient, or we can choose our own way. If we choose our own way, God may choose someone else to fulfill His plan, and you would miss out on the blessing and possibly change the end result. Mordecai said to Esther, "For if you remain silent at this time, relief and deliverance for the Jews will arise from another place, but you and your father's family will perish" (4:14a). Esther was in a difficult position. She knew what Haman was wanting to do to the Jews and she needed to warn the king. She was the queen, and the king loved her, but in those days, you couldn't go to the king unannounced, so she had to be clever and strategize. She asked for a meeting with not only the king but also with Haman. She fixed them dinner and then asked to serve them again another night which they agreed. Haman was so happy when he left the first feast, but it quickly changed when he saw Mordecai and he wanted to kill him. His wife and friends convinced him to build a gallows and put Mordecai and all the Jews on it. So he had a seventy-five-foot gallows built.

Here is where I love to see how God's timing works. The second thing that I will continually talk about is that God goes before us and prepares the way. We need to be faithful to His calling but also recognize His work when we see it. Esther's story is all about perfect timing and God's hand directing it all. In Esther 6, the king can't sleep so he had his daily chronicles (what he had done for the day) read to him. He heard about Mordecai saving his life from his two guards and asked if they had honored him for that. The reader said no. At that exact moment, Haman was walking through the courtyard to come talk to the king about hanging Mordecai. He came in and the king asked him, "What should be done for a man that the king wants to honor?" (6:6). Well, Haman was very full of himself and thought it was for him, so he suggested a lavish parade through town dressed in the king's finest and announce through town, "This is what is done for the man the king delights to honor" (6:9). The king said, "Great idea! Go, do this for Mordecai."

I can just imagine the devastation and humiliation that Haman felt because not only did he have to get it all together but also he had to be the herald that did the announcing. After that, he ran home in shame because he knew he was in trouble. But then the king's eunuch came and said it was time for dinner. I'm sure he had no appetite at that moment, but he went as he was commanded.

Esther had a nice spread of food waiting, and after they finished eating, the king asked Esther again, "What is your request? Even up to half the kingdom and it will be granted" (7:2). She boldly asked to have her life and the lives of her people spared. The king was enraged when Esther pointed out that Haman wanted them dead, and Haman was terrified. The king left their presence to cool down, but Haman stayed behind to beg for his life. When the king came back, he accused Haman of trying to molest the queen, so immediately, he and his family were hanged from the very gallows that he had built.

Perfect timing or God's timing? Yes. God's timing is perfect. Daily, I see how God's timing plays into our lives. He does go before us to prepare the way. His plan, whether we choose to be a part of it or not, will happen. But if He has chosen you to be a part of it, then not only will He go ahead of you to prepare the way, but also He will stand beside you as your support and guide. Then He will stand behind you and guard your back. Ask God to open your eyes to opportunities that He has already set in place, and then join in to see His glory magnified. You won't be disappointed, and I can guarantee blessings will flow as God is glorified.

Day 4

Gideon: Cautiously Obedient

How much proof do you need to know if something is true or false? Gideon was a questioner. He saw the angel of God face-to-face and did not die. Right after that, God said to tear down the Asherah pole to Baal, but he was afraid of the people, so he did it in the dark of night. When the people found out what he did, they changed his name to Jeru-Babel which means "Let Baal contend with him since he broke down Baal's altar" (Judges 6:32). Of course, nothing happened to him, but the name stuck with the people.

That reminds me of nicknames we gather through our lives. Some stick and give new meaning to our character, or it becomes a stigma we'd like to forget. For Gideon, this was a stigma that he had to live down. But he kept listening to God.

Gideon kept asking for signs as to whether what he heard was true. The first sign came when he wanted to bring an offering and set it before him, but he had to get everything prepared first. God said, "I will wait for you to return" (Judges 6:18). That happened to me at Whitestone when God was sharing things with me about my future and I wanted to write it down. God said, "I will wait for you to return." That was an amazing time in my life and quite a milestone for me. It was a milestone for Gideon as well because when he returned, the angel of God told him how to prepare the meat and bread, then once the angel set it on fire, he was gone. He made an altar there and in the place of the Asherah pole. Then their enemies started to advance on them. Gideon needed more reassurance that they would have victory, so he put out a fleece twice. He asked God to make the fleece wet and the ground dry in the morning, and it happened. Then he asked for the fleece to be dry and the ground wet the next morning, and it happened. Gideon's confidence grew. He took his men and prepared for battle, and God said, "You have too many men. Let's weed them out" (Judges 7:2). So Gideon said if anyone was too scared to fight, it was okay to go home. Then twenty-two thousand men went home, but ten thousand stayed. God said that was still too many. So he had the men go to the river, and those who brought the water to their mouth with their hand stayed., and those who lapped the water like an animal went home. Only three hundred remained. Now God was happy with that number and knew Israel wouldn't get the glory for the victory.

They divided up in sets of one hundred, and God told Gideon that He would deliver them, but since he was such a skeptic, he could take someone with him to overhear what they were talking about in the Amorite camp. Sure enough, he went and they were talking about how Gideon would be victorious over their camp. Gideon was so excited that he worshipped God and ran back and put the teams together for the attack. When they surrounded the camp and smashed their jugs and blew their horns, then the Amorites turned on themselves, and all they had to do was walk in.

God will fight your battles for you. God is patient enough to see our skepticism. He will show Himself in various ways to prove He is God, but He is not a circus act and will not do things for show.

God had a purpose with Gideon. He wanted to bring Israel back to Himself, and He knew Gideon was the man for the job. Gideon was not so sure of himself, but the more God revealed himself to Gideon, the bolder he became. Peace reigned for forty years. But as soon as he was dead, they went right back to worshipping Baal, and the cycle began again.

Who do we have our faith in? Leaders of this world or God? If it's leaders of this world, then they will fail us every time, but if our faith is in God, He will show us the way and protect us at the same time. We are living in very uncertain times, but God said, "Take heart; I have overcome the world" (John 16:33). If you need a sign, ask for one. He just may give you one. But when He does, be prepared for what happens next. God may choose to use you to let His glory shine. Will you choose to obey or walk away? There's always a choice.

Day 5

Daniel: Obedience Is a Choice

In the majority of Bible studies that I have done over the years, choice as stated on earlier days is a recurring theme. Each person in the Bible had a choice to live for God or not. Daniel was no different. He had two paths laid out for him: choose to eat of the king's food or choose the food that God laid out for him to eat. Another choice he had was to pray only to the king daily or pray to God daily. Each had a consequence. Each had a reward. But for Daniel, he had to choose which consequence was greater and which reward was greater.

In Daniel 1, Daniel and his friends were told to eat of the king's table so that they would be strong men, ready to fight in the king's army. But they inquired of the guard to "test their servants for 10 days: give nothing but vegetables to eat and water to drink. Then compare their appearance with that of the young men who ate the royal food and treat them in accordance to what they see" (Daniel 1:12–14). The guard agreed, and at the end of ten days, they looked healthier and better nourished than any of the young men who ate the royal food. So the guard changed the diet of all the young men to be like Daniel and his friends (Daniel 1:15–16). Because of this, "Daniel and his friends were given knowledge and understanding of all kinds of literature and learning. And Daniel could understand various dreams of all kinds" (Daniel 1:17).

With this gift, Daniel became highly favored with the kings, but the other leaders didn't like him at all. They wanted him killed, so they trapped the king into making a decree that everyone could only pray/worship the king, and if they didn't, then they would be thrown into the lion's den. Choices again for Daniel were really no choice at all. Daniel had been faithful to God, and God had blessed him continually, and he had no doubt that He would continue. So "three times a day he got down on his knees and prayed to God just as he had done before in front of the open windows facing Jerusalem" (Daniel 6:10). The leaders found him as they knew they would and brought him before the king to be thrown into the lion's den. The king was saddened but did as he had decreed hoping for a different result. The king came back the next day, and Daniel was still living with no wounds at all. The leaders who falsely accused Daniel were thrown into the lions' den and eaten before they hit the floor. The king then declared and issued a new decree that all people would worship Daniel's God from that day forward.

God used Daniel because he was faithful and strong enough to believe that his God was bigger than any person or situation he was in. We too have that same choice. Every day, we wake up and decide to start our day with prayer and Bible study or not. We decide to eat healthy or not. We decide to watch uplifting things or not. We decide to get in on downgrading others or not. We decide. We decide. We decide. There are only two choices in life, and you have to choose to be obedient to God or obedient to the world. Both have consequences. Both have rewards. Which is greater for you?

"But if serving the Lord seems undesirable to you, then choose for yourselves this day whom you will serve, but as for me and my household, we will serve the Lord" (Joshua 24:15).

Section 2: Bad Decision Makers

Day 1

Cain versus Abel: Pride versus Obedience

If you do what is right, will you not be accepted? But if you do not do what is right, sin is crouching at your door; it desires to have you, but you must master it.

—Genesis 4:7

This was said to Cain after God blessed Abel's offering and not his. We have a gauge within us to know what is right and what is wrong, and we have a choice. Choose wisely and God is pleased. Choose selfishly and God may punish you. But one thing is for certain: He will not be pleased.

Abel was a hunter and shepherd. Cain was a keeper of the soil, but I'm not exactly sure what his produce was. Their task was to offer God their best. "Cain brought *some* of the fruits of the soil as an offering to the Lord and Abel brought fat portions from *some* of the firstborn of his flock" (Genesis 4:3–4; italics mine). Each of them brought *some*, but the *some* for each signified something different. For Cain, it was a thing he had to do, so he went to the fruits of his field and basically said, "Okay, what can I take for an offering? It really doesn't matter what I bring. These fruits will do." And he gathered up random fruits and took them.

For Abel, it was an important part of his life. When the firstborn were born, he looked at them all and probably said, "God deserves my best. The fat portion of these are my best. I'll take those."

For God, He saw beyond the offering. He saw the heart of the givers. He saw the nonchalant attitude of Cain's gift, and He saw the love and care of Abel's gift. God blessed Abel and reprimanded Cain.

Cain was angry and jealous which caused him to take Abel out into the field and kill him. Just like with his parents (Adam and Eve) when they hid from his sight, Cain tried to cover up what he did when God asked where Abel was. He said, "Am I my brother's keeper?" God cursed Cain for the rest of his life to being a restless wanderer, and no one was allowed to kill him or they would be cursed even more.

How you give to the Lord is all about you attitude. Do you give obediently because God says to and you want to do so or give disgruntledly because you have to? The blessing of God comes from the outflow of the heart. He desires your obedience so that in the end He is glorified and pleased. The choice is yours.

Who are you more like? Cain or Abel?

Day 2

The Tower of Babel: The Ripple Effect of Disobedience

Obedience comes from not trying to one-up God and become like Him or even to receive higher glory or recognition more than God. Yet, from Satan on down to the people of Earth, it is tried again and again. And then the all-knowing, all-seeing God Himself comes along and says, "No. Not going to happen." That is what happened with the Tower of Babel. The people got so comfortable with each other and truly got along with each other. They thought they were something. "They said, 'Come, let us build ourselves a city, with a tower that reaches to the heavens, so that we may make a name for ourselves and not be scattered over the face of the whole earth'" (Genesis 11:4). Wonder what would've happened if they had not built the tower. Would we have all been able to understand each other from any part of the world? Who knows? Because the ripple effect off that one action affected the rest of the world for the rest of time.

The Lord saw what they were doing and decided that this wasn't going to happen. "So the Lord scattered them from there over all the earth, and they stopped building the city. That is why it is called Babel—because there the Lord confused the language of the whole world. From there the Lord scattered them over the face of the whole earth" (Genesis 11:8–9).

"Pride goes before destruction, a haughty spirit before a fall" (Proverbs 16:18). What makes people do what they want to do when they want to do it? Pride. The people that were building the tower had such a pride. They had designed a new way to build buildings that were more durable, and so they thought, "Since we work so well together, let's build this tower to the heavens and we'll never be scattered over the earth" (Genesis 11:4). The comical notion to this is that they thought their tower was so large and tall, but yet "God had to come down from heaven just to see it" (Genesis 11:5). Which shows what we think is monstrously huge, God sees as the size of a Lego building block.

What we do affects others. It may not seem like it at the time, but it does. The Tower of Babel brought about different languages and different people groups. It also showed how easily our pride gets in the way of serving God. And how easily God can take away what we think is most important.

Seek His face. Follow His ways. Make ripple effects for God's glory today and not your own.

Day 3

The Sin of Achan

Have you ever done an experiment with a glass of water and one drop of food coloring? What was clear and pure, with one drop of food coloring becomes tainted and murky. This is what happened with the Israelites and Achan. The Israelites had just had a major victory in defeating the city of Jericho with Joshua as their leader. They had spared Rahab and her family, taken their plunder, and burned the city. They were victorious. At least that was until greed and covetousness set in for one individual named Achan.

Achan saw "a beautiful robe from Babylon, 200 shekels of silver and a wedge of gold weighing 50 shekels" (Joshua 7:21), and he had to have them. So he hid them among his things thinking no one would notice because they had taken so much. Yet God knew and saw everything, so "God's anger burned against Israel" (Joshua 7:1). God didn't take it out on Achan alone nor did He tell Joshua what happened until he tried to fight the city of Ai and was defeated. Joshua was devastated at the loss, "tore his clothes and fell face down before the Lord" (Joshua 7:6) and asked why would God bring them across the Jordan just to destroy them. Even then, God didn't straight out say, Achan has sinned, and I'm taking it out on everyone. He just said, "Israel has sinned and broken the covenant which I commanded them to keep. They have taken some of the devoted things; they have stolen, they have lied, they have put them with their own possessions. That is why the Israelites cannot stand against their enemies. I will not be with you anymore unless you destroy whatever among you is devoted to destruction" (Joshua 7:11–12).

Joshua brought in tribe by tribe until it got down to family by family and then man by man then down to Achan. Achan confessed, "It is true! I have sinned against the Lord, the God of Israel" (Joshua 7:20). Joshua took him and his family and his livestock, stoned them, and then burned them in a field in order to restore Israel in God's eyes. At that point, "God turned from his fierce anger" (Joshua 7:26).

Isn't it amazing what one person's actions will do for the lives of many? We have seen that in full while being subject to this quarantine. We have seen where one virus in Wuhan, China, affected the world in rapid succession, and in turn, the entire world basically shut down, and lives were destroyed in the process.

In turn, people's eyes have been opened to what is "essential" in life, and things we thought were most important were taken away. God has told us time and time again through Scripture to turn back to Him and we are too busy or too focused on other things, so He has had to get our attention through other means. "When I shut up the heavens so that there is no rain or command locusts to devour the land or send a plague among the people, if my people who are called by My name, will humble themselves and pray and seek my face and turn from their wicked ways, then will I hear from heaven and will forgive their sin and heal their land" (2 Chronicles 7:13–14).

God has watched our world destroy itself through the years of unfaithfulness, and it's time to turn back and humble ourselves before Him and pray and seek His face and turn away from all wickedness so that He will forgive us and heal our land. It's time to become a clear glass of water again. "Create in me a clean heart, O God and restore a right spirit within me" (Psalm 51:10).

Day 4

Samson: Naiveté Brings Disobedience

I've had friends so blinded by love that they can't see the issues right in front of their faces. Even if you were to point out the problems, they would laugh and deny it completely. Samson was that blind when it came to women. When he loved a woman, he put his full trust in them even though each woman tried to destroy him over and over again.

From before he was conceived, Samson was set apart to be different. His mom couldn't drink wine or any fermented drink while pregnant with Samson so that he would never have a taste for it when he was born. The angel of the Lord was very specific to Manoah and his wife that Samson's hair would never be cut and he would never drink wine and his strength would be powerful. He had it all; therefore, he thought he was invincible. With his hair not cut, he was but his ego always seemed to get in the way.

At his wedding feast, he told a riddle to the Philistines and gave them seven days to figure it out, but they couldn't. So they had his new wife try to coax it out of him, and she even used the wiles of "You don't really love me if you can't trust me with the answer" line. For three days, she hounded him, and he finally gave in to giving her the answer. She immediately told the Philistines who in turn told Samson. He was angry and "the Spirit of the Lord came upon him.

He went down to Ashkelon, struck down 30 of their men, stripped them of their belongings and gave the clothing to the one who solved the riddle" (Judges 14:19). Samson's dad gave his new wife to Samson's friend because of the betrayal.

Samson had amazing strength. He killed a lion with his bare hands. He killed one thousand men with the jawbone of a donkey, and people began to wonder. How do we subdue such a man? He fell in love with Delilah who was his downfall. Three times she asked him how he got his strength, and three times she tried what he claimed brought him strength. Each time, he got out of the bindings that held him as if it were nothing. Lesson not learned, with Delilah scheming against him, he finally told her the truth. The Philistines came back one more time, and this time, they succeeded in subduing him because Delilah had cut his hair. The Philistines gouged out his eyes, and he was blind for the rest of his days in prison.

The people wanted him to entertain them now that he had no strength before he was offered as a sacrifice to their god, Dagon. So he asked to be placed between two pillars in the front of the temple. He prayed for strength one last time to destroy the Philistines, and God granted his request. He said, "Let me die with the Philistines! Then he pushed with all his might, and down came the temple on the rulers and all the people in it. Thus, he killed many more when he died than when he lived" (Judges 16:30).

Arrogance or naiveté? Yes. A little bit of both. Samson had it all, yet that was his downfall. He trusted in the wrong people too many times. How many times do we do the same? The voices of the whiners and complainers become so great that you just give in time and time again and each one brings a little bit more destruction. Until finally, it destroys everything that God has set out for you to do. Too morbid? Maybe. But it happens so much more than not these days.

It is hard to hear the voice of God over the world at times, and those voices become like screeching wheels. We can't let the screeching wheels become the ruling factors in our lives. Take time to step back away from your situations to see the full picture, to be able to hear God better and listen for His voice again. Destruction waits at your door if you aren't careful.

Day 5

The Rich Man Who Walked Away

You cannot serve both God and money.
—Matthew 6:24b

We live in a world of easy access to anything our heart desires, and oftentimes, those desires become greater than our desire to serve God. When that happens, what/who we worship replaces God's place in our hearts. We are a society of idol makers. We need something tangible to see, feel, and hear in order for our life to be fulfilled. God's greatest commandment above all things is to "Love the Lord with all your heart, mind, soul and strength" (Mark 12:30). People are always asking what God's will is for their life, and it is plainly written: love God, love people, and share the Gospel with others. If we do that, we will be glorifying God with our lives.

There was a rich man that had a problem with that. He loved his money and probably worked really hard to earn it. However, Jesus knew his heart. The man wanted justification from Jesus that he had done enough to get into heaven. He wanted to work his way into heaven instead of freely giving all himself to Jesus. Here's the story from Matthew 19:16–30.

> Just then a man came up to Jesus and asked, "Teacher, what good thing must I do to get eternal life?"

"Why do you ask me about what is good?" Jesus replied. "There is only One who is good. If you want to enter life, keep the commandments."

"Which ones?" he inquired.

Jesus replied, "You shall not murder, you shall not commit adultery, you shall not steal, you shall not give false testimony, honor your father and mother,' and 'love your neighbor as yourself."

"All these I have kept," the young man said. "What do I still lack?"

Jesus answered, "If you want to be perfect, go, sell your possessions and give to the poor, and you will have treasure in heaven. Then come, follow me."

When the young man heard this, he went away sad, because he had great wealth.

Then Jesus said to his disciples, "Truly I tell you, it is hard for someone who is rich to enter the kingdom of heaven. Again, I tell you, it is easier for a camel to go through the eye of a needle than for someone who is rich to enter the kingdom of God."

When the disciples heard this, they were greatly astonished and asked, "Who then can be saved?"

Jesus looked at them and said, "With man this is impossible, but with God all things are possible."

Peter answered him, "We have left everything to follow you! What then will there be for us?"

Jesus said to them, "Truly I tell you, at the renewal of all things, when the Son of Man sits on his glorious throne, you who have followed me will also sit on twelve thrones, judging the

> twelve tribes of Israel. And everyone who has left houses or brothers or sisters or father or mother or wife or children or fields for my sake will receive a hundred times as much and will inherit eternal life. But many who are first will be last, and many who are last will be first."

The rich man walked away sad because he knew he couldn't do what Jesus was asking of him. So, in looking back through the Ten Commandments, he broke the very first one in not having any idols before God. Money is an idol if it is more important to you than serving God. Anything placed above God in our mind or life is an idol.

It doesn't mean we have to live the life of a monk. God has given us the ability to use things for His glory. We need to be thankful for what God has blessed us with but not to let it become more important than God or He could choose to take it from us. Look at the story of the man who stored up years' worth of grain in his storehouses instead of sharing them. Jesus called him a fool and said that his life would be taken that night.

We must use what God has given us for His glory not our own. It will make for a better and more fulfilled life.

What's more important to you? God or what you have? COVID-19 has brought out a new side to people, which is both a positive and a negative: negative being that people are hoarding up all that they can so they don't run out of anything, just in case even the grocery stores close; positive being that people are giving more of themselves, more of their time (because they have it now), and more of their "stuff" (money, supplies). I've even seen more scripture posted, more sermons preached, more encouragement, and simply more of what it is to be a community (without getting too close, of course). Yet, people still don't believe. People would rather do good and hope that it's enough to get them into heaven than to call on the name of the Lord to be their Savior. This was the problem with the rich young man. He had the wealth to give and was probably a great philanthropist, but to give it *all* away? That was too great a sacrifice, and Jesus knew that. Jesus knew that money and power were what was most important to him, so even though he followed the Ten Commandments to a point, Jesus knew that his love for money was greater than his love to serve Jesus.

I love the picture of a camel going through the eye of a needle. Throughout my growing up years, I always thought it meant an actual needle which, of course, would've been impossible, but as I grew up and began to understand more about the terrain of the area, I realized that there is a mountain pass called the "eye of the needle." This place is very narrow, and only one person at a time can walk through it. Camels are too big and wouldn't fit, so if you have camels or an entourage, you would have to take the long way around instead of the shortcut through the "eye of the needle." So the disciples understood how difficult it was for this man to obey. However, despite the feeling of impossibility of giving everything up to follow Jesus, if he had gone a step further and done what Jesus had said, then who knows what could've happened.

Jesus said, "With man, being saved is impossible but with God all things are possible" (Mark 10:27). When we see no way, God says, "I am the Way. Follow Me." The rich man walked away before he saw the way because he loved his stuff more. What about you? Whose way are you following: your own or God's?

Section 3: Evidence of Obedience

Day 1

Balaam: Fear Makes You Desperate

Balak, king of Moab, had been watching what Israel was doing to other countries, and now the Amorites had been defeated, and the Moabites were scared. *Terrified* is the word used in the NIV. In his reign, he knew that Balaam had the ability to hear from God but wanted his own agenda carried out instead. So he sent men to ask Balaam to come curse Israel so they couldn't attack Moab. Balaam said, "Spend the night here and I'll let you know what God says in the morning" (Numbers 22:8).

In today's society, we are quick to make a decision about anything and everything. "There isn't time to wait" is always a response when really that is what we have in this moment…time. Time to read God's Word. Time to be still before the Lord and listen. Time to worship Him. When we take the time, He will guide us in the right direction. I'm a big supporter of early morning devotions, but that's not for everyone, I get that. However, when your day gets rolling, it's hard to roll back the day and stop. Take the time because God desires to share His heart with you. He desires to lead, guide, and direct us in His ways.

Balaam went back to Balak's men and said, "God told me not go because He can't put a curse on a people that are already blessed" (Numbers 22:12). The men went back, and Balak wasn't happy and sent even more men that were "more numerous and more distinguished than the first" (Numbers 22:15) and asked him again.

"Balaam answered them, 'Even if Balak gave me his palace filled with silver and gold, I couldn't do anything great or small to go beyond the command of the Lord my God. Now stay here tonight and I'll see what the Lord has to say and I'll let you know tomorrow'" (Numbers 22:18–19).

Waiting on the Lord is hard, but when you get an answer of no or wait, it sometimes gets a little harder because it is hard to accept. God has plans that we know nothing about, and our job is to trust that plan above what we see. "Faith is being sure of what we hope for and certain of what we do not see" (Hebrews 11:1). We need to trust that God, Who made the universe, is here watching over us and taking care of us. It's hard during this time of unrest, but if we listen and act accordingly, He will show us the way.

God told Balaam to go with them but say only what God has him say. Tomorrow, we see how his donkey comes into being a part of the story. Stay faithful.

Day 2

Balaam: Stay True to What God Says

Now that Balaam agreed to go, "The Lord was angry that he went" (Numbers 22:22). This verse has always confused me. After all, God said for him to go, right? Actually, God said not to go the first time, and "God does not chew his cud twice" (as my husband says). If God says no, He doesn't typically change His mind just because you ask again. He may allow you to go, but He won't like it. Balaam was allowed to talk one on one with the Lord which most didn't have. So when Balaam asked God the same question again about going to curse Israel, His answer was the same: "I can't curse what has already been blessed." Then God added to His statement, "But since these men have asked again and you want to go, then go. However, do only what I tell you" (Numbers 22:20). What is the definition of insanity? Doing the same thing over and over again expecting different results. The king of Moab figured if he brought in more distinguished men and the promise of wealth, that would win over Balaam and ultimately God. However, what does God need with earthly wealth when He owns the cattle on a thousand hills?

How many times do we get frustrated with others when they ask the same question over and over again as if they can't grasp the concept? For me, I find myself being the persistent questioner, and I see the frustrations on the faces of the ones having to answer. Thankfully,

God is patient. He is a protector. He leads us faithfully. But sometimes, we are too blind to see it. Thus, God used Balaam's donkey.

Balaam got on his donkey and began riding toward Moab, but because God was angry at Balaam, He sent an angel with a sword down to block his path. The only problem was that Balaam couldn't see him but the donkey could. So each time the angel got in their path, the donkey would veer off the road, and Balaam, each time, would beat the donkey until he moved again. Finally, the third time, the donkey just sat down and wouldn't budge. Balaam again began beating the donkey.

> "Finally, God opened the mouth of the donkey and said, "What have I done to you to make you beat me these three times?" Balaam answered the donkey, "You have made a fool of me! If I had a sword in my hand, I would kill you right now." The donkey said to Balaam, "Am I not your own donkey, which you have always ridden to this day? Have I been in the habit of doing this to you?" "No," he said. Then the Lord opened the eyes of Balaam and he saw the angel of the Lord standing in the road with his sword drawn. So he bowed low and fell face down." (Numbers 22:28–31).

Sometimes, God has to use extraordinary measures for us to be aware of God's truth. And if we aren't faithful to what God says, then He will use other means to get our attention, like a talking donkey, to get us to focus once again. Is God blocking your path right now from going in a certain direction but you keep trying to press forward despite the obstacles? Maybe God wants you to take a step back to reevaluate what you are doing. God loves speaking with His own, we just have to be willing to listen and obey. "His ways nor His thoughts are like our ways or thoughts," but His plan is perfect, and we need to listen to it. He sees the end. This is where faith becomes strongest. Trust in Him. He will never lead you astray.

Day 3

Balaam: Once Reminded, Stay True

Do you cave easily to the pressures of those around you, or do you stick with your convictions and stand strong despite the opposition? Balaam had a choice: listen to the Lord or cave to Balak. After the experience on the road with a talking donkey and an angel with a sword, I would feel more compelled to stand a little taller in my stance because I would know the power of the Lord was with me. Thankfully, Balaam also felt that same conviction, but Balak was quite the persistent one.

As we read about Balak, he shows a high amount of fear for being conquered by Israel and only is thinking of himself and his kingdom as opposed to God's plans. He tried three times to get Balaam to curse Israel, and each time, it came with a blessing instead. Balaam insisted every time that he could only say what God told him to say and every time God would say, "I can't curse something I've already blessed."

The first oracle of Balaam was made at Bamoth Baal. He told Balak to build seven altars and prepare seven bulls and seven rams for the offering. This is not a quick go-to-the-market-for-meat task. This takes time and energy. So Balaam goes to God while Balak waits at the offering. Balaam comes back after talking with the Lord and shares the news. Balak gets a little more desperate and takes Balaam to the field of Zophim on top of Pisgah. Balaam makes him create seven more altars with a ram and bull on each and comes back with the same news and a reprimand from God to Balak saying, "God is not a man that he should lie, nor a son of man that he should change his mind" (Numbers 23:19). Balak became fully desperate by now. The first two places only showed parts of the Israel people, but now he took Balaam to the top of Peor where he could see all the people of Israel. Balaam told him to build seven more altars with seven more bulls and rams. This time, when he went to the Lord, he came back to look out over the people, and as the Spirit of the Lord came upon him, he blessed them.

> "Balak was so angry with Balaam. He said, "Leave at once and go home! I said I would reward you but the Lord has prevented that from happening." Balaam answered, "I told your messengers, even if Balak offered me a place filled with silver and gold, I could not do anything on my own accord, good or bad to go beyond the command of the Lord—and I must say only what the Lord says.
>
> Now I am going back to my people, but come, let me warn you of what this people will do to your people in days to come" (Numbers 24:12–14).

And he proceeds to share the destruction of Moab.

God is not one to be messed with. If He says "No," then take the no as a sign of protection. If He says "Yes," then take the yes as a sign of blessing. If He says, "Wait" or gives no answer yet, then know that God's timing is perfect and He will reveal Himself in time—we just need to wait. But if God says "No" and you keep pushing your agenda, it won't change His mind, and it might make Him say as He did with Balaam, "I said No but since you keep asking, if you want to go then go, but my mind will not change still." In fact, sometimes, if we persist even when God says "No," our frustrations will grow immensely because we are trying to fit a square peg in a round hole.

Our job is to seek the Lord, listen to the Lord, and obey the Lord. If we try any other way, we too may be facing a talking donkey to get our attention.

Day 4

Joseph: The Later Years

Don't be afraid. Am I in the place of God? You intended to harm me, but God intended it for good to accomplish what is now being done.
—Genesis 50:19–20

Joseph went through so much in his life from being sold into slavery to being wrongly accused so he was put in jail to becoming a leader in Pharaoh's house to having the knowledge to save a whole country from famine to reuniting and reconciling with his family. Kelly Clarkson's song, "What Doesn't Kill You Makes You Stronger," really holds true for Joseph. He could've given up or given in to many of the pressures of life, but he didn't. He stayed true to God, and God honored him in return. So many of us quit things before we get started because we know it's going to be difficult or we don't want to put in the effort. However, Joseph is the epitome of what happens when we obey. God unveiled Joseph's life to him at the end, and he was able to share it with his brothers who were still scared that he would retaliate. After explaining all that happened to him to his brothers, he said, "God sent me ahead of you to preserve for you a remnant on earth and to save your lives by a great deliverance. So, then it was not you who sent me here but God" (Genesis 45:7–8).

I have always prayed, "God, go before me to prepare the way. Stand beside me and be my support. Walk behind me to guard my back." It occurred to me today that He often uses us to be the ones to go before others to prepare their way. I've had people ask on occasion, "Why am I having to go through this?" And my response is, "Maybe this journey is to help someone that is coming behind you." God knows our strengths, and He sees the ones that are strong enough to lean on God through the tough times, and He knows the ones that need a physical guide to get through the same situation later on. So the strong leaders lead the way despite the tough circumstances.

Joseph leaned heavily on God, and He saw Joseph through some incredibly tough times. And because of his obedience, he became a leader. He didn't let the circumstances break him. He let God mold him, and because of that, everyone was saved during the famine. Don't be so consumed with the circumstances that you miss the blessings. Lean on God to make you stronger, and the evidence of your obedience will be evident to all.

Day 5

The Rocks Will Cry Out: Be Obedient or God Will Use Someone Else

Blessed is the king who comes in the name of the Lord! Peace in heaven and glory in the highest!
—Luke 19:38

As Jesus was traveling into Jerusalem, all the followers of Him were so excited to see Him. So much so that they gathered on the streets like a parade to welcome Him into town. They put their cloaks on the ground so that his donkey wouldn't have to walk on the dusty road, and they waved palm branches as He rode by. According to amazingbibletimes.com, "There was common practice in the ancient world to welcome home a king or war hero by laying out a path of branches for him to ride/walk on—similar to rolling out the red carpet today." The people of Jerusalem saw Him as their king and were excited to see Him. The Pharisees, however, were not happy to see all this fanfare for Jesus. They didn't see it as necessary and were quite offended by it. Basically, they were jealous.

They told Jesus to have them stop the silliness of laying cloaks on the ground, singing and waving palm branches, but Jesus simply said, "If they keep quiet, the stones will cry out" (Luke 19:40). We were made to praise God, and if we don't, then God will find other ways for His creation to praise Him. I remember when the boys were little, they did a skit at church called, "Rocks will cry out." They were supposed to be two rocks on the ground, and they were being observant of all that was going on around them. Then all of the sudden, they said, "What's happening?" And they began to praise Him with "hosannas." They talked about how the people had grown silent in talking about Jesus, and when that happened, the rocks began to praise Him.

Crazy as that sounds of rocks crying out in praise to God, according to Jesus, He would use them in a heartbeat because God must be praised. He must be honored. He must be revered. If we don't do it, He will get someone/something that will. In today's times of churches being closed, our voices need to rise even more. We need others to know who is in control of this world. Fear has no hold on us! If we aren't faithful then beware, the rocks in your driveway may break out in song. Praise Him today.

Day 6

Two Sons: Word versus Actions

I know that I'm not the only one that tells her sons to do something, they say okay, and then it doesn't get done. I know this because Jesus mentions it in a parable and He doesn't do things randomly. He always has a purpose for those that were there with Him and those reading today. It's not just our kids that do this, but we do it too. We'll agree to something then back out at the last minute or forget altogether. It happens.

However, that is not a good excuse and should be reanalyzed. So let's do that. In this week, we are talking about the evidence of obedience. People will know us by our fruits. If they see us as dependable, they will give us more responsibility. If we are seen as less dependable, then we will receive less to do because they know it won't get done if given to us to do—just look at the story of talents (Matthew 25:14–30).

Jesus knew His audience well, not just their looks and the outside appearance, they showed everyone else, but also He knew their heart and inner thoughts. He knew the ones asking Him questions had the look of being the spiritual leaders but in their hearts despised Jesus. So he told the story of two sons (Matthew 21:28–31a).

> There was a man who had two sons. He went to the first and said, "Son, go and work today in the vineyard."

> "I will not," he answered, but later he changed his mind and went.
>
> Then the father went to the other son and said the same thing. He answered, "I will, sir," but he did not go.
>
> "Which of the two did what his father wanted?" "The first," they answered. Jesus said to them, "Truly I tell you, the tax collectors and the prostitutes are entering the kingdom of God ahead of you."

The father had one desire: for both his sons to go work in the field. The field of today could be the field of souls—sharing the gospel, bringing more to Him daily. Some go to church, do the right things as a front, but back home or out and about town, their lives reflect something completely opposite. Then there are those that have fought against God for so long and then realize that following Jesus is the only way, receive Jesus into lives, and share Him with everyone. Jesus said, "I tell you the truth, the tax collectors and prostitutes are entering the kingdom of God ahead of you. For John came to show you the way of righteousness, and you did not believe Him but the tax collectors and prostitutes did. And even after you saw this, you did not repent and believe Him" (Matthew 21:31b–32).

God desires you to serve Him and share Him with everyone. Are you going to be like the second son and say okay but never do it? Or are you going to be like the first son and finally obey and share Jesus with everyone you meet? The beauty is we don't always have to use words. Actions are just as powerful, and God will still work through you.

Jesus said, "Let your yes be yes and your no be no." We must do what we say we will do. Obedience comes with action. Sometimes, it may come with sacrifice. Sometimes, it may take courage. But God is calling us all to obey. It will look different to every single person, but the end result should be the same for all, saying yes to God and following through the commitment. Being faithful to our promises is crucial to a productive and fulfilling life in Christ.

Day 7

Disciples: Evidence of Obedience

Come, follow Me.
—Matthew 9:9

It is a simple command, yet it held such power. Think about it: Peter was told he would be a fisher of men and dropped his nets—a full, overflowing catch at that—and followed. In John 1:35–51, these new disciples kept asking questions of Jesus, and He simply said, "Come and you will see" (John 1:39). Every one of the disciples left their livelihoods to live for Jesus.

- Andrew, Peter, James, and John were fishermen.
- Matthew was a tax collector.
- Simon the Zealot was a member of the Zealots party.
- The other disciples' occupations were not well known, but each of them gave up their daily lives to follow Jesus.

The group of twelve plus Jesus were together for three years, and in that time, the disciples witnessed firsthand miracle after miracle but, until God opened their spiritual eyes to see Jesus for who He really was, did they actually understand who Jesus was. They had seen the feeding of the five thousand and were sitting in a boat in the middle of the lake in the midst of a storm and didn't realize that the one who controlled the weather and seas was in the boat sleeping, yet when push came to shove, they woke him up, and Jesus calmed the storm.

They saw Him crucified and buried and then hid in fear that they would come after them too. But as soon as Mary told them the tomb was empty, they took off to see for themselves. When Jesus came to them on the beach after the resurrection and gave them instruction on what they would be doing for the rest of their lives, they finally started to understand. When they met together in a room afterward and the Holy Spirit came upon them, their worlds became clear in what they were to do.

Obey. Each one of them had three years of training from the perfect teacher. They went out boldly proclaiming His Word for the rest of their lives. Each of them died a martyr's death in one way or another, but the threat of death didn't stop them from being obedient. They had trained for these moments. And the evidence was clearly seen for thousands of years on. They didn't seek glory or fame. Their only goal was to share God's Word with everyone.

God wants to see the evidence of obedience in us. He doesn't want us to seek glory and fame; He just wants us to be faithful and obedient. God will receive the glory, and we will see the effects of obedience. It's not an easy road, but it is the most important. Study and then go. Be obedient.

Section 4: You: Obedient or Not? The Story of Jehoshaphat

Day 1

Asa: Jehoshaphat's Father

Jehoshaphat's father, Asa, started out as a faithful believer. In 1 Kings 15:9–24, we read about how "he did what was right in the eyes of the Lord just as David did" (v. 11). He got rid of prostitutes and idols and cut down the Asherah pole that his grandmother, Maacah, had as the queen and he burned it in the Kidron Valley. However, he didn't get rid of the high places where people worshipped. But for his early years of reign, "his heart was fully committed to the Lord" (v. 14).

In fact, Azariah, son of Oded, had the spirit of the Lord come upon him to share some information with Asa. He said, "Listen to me, Asa, all Judah and Benjamin. The Lord is with you when you are with him. If you seek him, he will be found by you, but if you forsake him, he will forsake you" (2 Chronicles 15:2). Asa believed and got rid of all hindrances as stated above, and "there was no more war until the 35th year of Asa's reign" (15:19). And then things changed. Asa's heart changed, and He began to rely on the help of others instead of seeking God's direction. Asa had already been warned by Azariah of what would happen if he forsook God. So God, being true to His word, gave Hanani, the seer, some words of warning to give to Asa.

You see, Asa decided to make allies with Ben-Hadad, the king of Aram, and asked him to break his treaty with the king of Israel. Ben-Hadad agreed, and they conquered all the towns of Israel together.

Now that may seem like a good thing since they conquered opposing armies together; however, God was not in the fight with them. My husband said in a sermon, "Sometimes, something may be right but not the right timing." In Asa's case, we will never know if there was a right timing because he decided to get the consult of man over going to God first. When he did that, God sent Hanani, the seer, to him with a message regarding his future. In 2 Chronicles 16:7–9, Hanani said, "Because you relied on the King of Aram and not on the Lord your God, the army of the King of Aram has escaped from your hand…you have done a foolish thing and from now on you will be at war." During his thirty-five years with no war, God had delivered large armies such as the Cushites and Libyans into his hand with no problems, but he saw the army of Aram too big to handle, so he made them an ally. If he had gone to God first, then God would've fought for him.

God had said back in 15:2, "If you seek God, you will find Him. If you forsake God, He will forsake you." God lived up to His word and struck Asa's feet with a disease in his thirty-ninth year of reign, and even then, he did not seek the Lord. When Hanani had told him what God had said, "Asa was angry with the seer and put him in prison and brutally oppressed some of the people" (16:10). For the rest of his reign from the thirty-sixth year to his forty-first year, he was angry with the Lord, and he was constantly at war.

Imagine all the good that could've come from his reign as king if he continued to seek the Lord, but anger came in like a roaring lion and captured him. It is so easy to live in anger and bitterness and unfairness to how life treats you. It's not fun, but it's easy to get sucked into that world. God has said, "Vengeance is mine, I will repay" (Romans 12:19), which means that is not our problem to handle. If God wants to change a life through discipline, then He is God, and He is able. We are only able to see what we see so where we see things as unfair, God sees it as part of His ultimate plan, and we get to just watch him work.

Asa listened to God for thirty-five years and had no war. He processed the fact that God could be found in any situation as long as he called on God first and allowed God to take the lead in his life.

Asa believed that God had the power to do anything and saw it first-hand with the conquering of large armies easily. He acted on what God advised for thirty-five years, and the result was peace. Then it wasn't. And God removed His hand of protection, and his life was full of destruction and defeat until the end.

Peace or defeat? Which is better? Which do you live in at the moment? If you live in peace, that is fantastic! Congratulations! Continue to live in God's peace, His guidance, and His victory. It is a precious thing to find peace in the midst of a storm, one that can't be taken for granted.

For those living in defeat, why do you choose that direction? It is a choice. We have a God that is the victor over sin and death, and He desires to be victorious in your life as well. Instead, we choose our own path, our own desires, and our own self-pity, and then we are miserable. And we wonder why God is not helping us. God plainly said to Asa, "If you seek me, you will find me" (15:2). But Jesus also said in the New Testament, "Seek and you will find, ask and it shall be given, knock and the door will be opened to you" (Matthew 7:7). And yet we don't ask. We don't seek. We don't knock. And God stands back and waits. He is a patient God, but we miss the blessing when we don't listen, process, believe, and act because once we do, the result is victory. What are you waiting for?

Day 2

Godly Examples

Honor your father and your mother.
—Exodus 20:12

How often do you wonder as a parent if you are making a difference in the lives of your children? Do you ever wonder if they will imitate your bad habits or your good habits? Do you look at your children and pray that their decisions would be wise and their future mate will follow Christ as well? All these things run through my head constantly especially now that they are getting older and becoming their own men. My prayer is that they choose God above everything else and live for Him with their whole heart. If they do that, then everything should fall into the right alignment. We have told them on many occasions to be careful of what they say or do because even if we aren't there to see, they still have their heavenly Father watching.

Jehoshaphat had a front-row seat to watching a godly king reign his country, but he also had a front-row seat to watch that same king make bad decisions which changed his attitude, demeanor, and ultimately end his reign as king. So Jehoshaphat had a choice: which example was he going to follow? The godly example or the selfish example? Thankfully, he chose to be a godly king. "The Lord was with Jehoshaphat because in his early years he walked in the ways of his father David had followed" (2 Chronicles 17:3). Notice it said "in his early years" which is when Asa was following the Lord completely because there were thirty-five years of no war. So, during this time, Jehoshaphat was getting godly training from Asa on how to lead the people with the Lord as the leader. Jehoshaphat listened to the teachings of the Lord. As he listened, he began to walk in the ways of the Lord by processing everything he learned and put it all in to practice. He watched the godly Asa and the destructive Asa and believed that following the Lord was the best way to rule the people. So, when it was his turn to step up to be king, he acted under the godly rule, and the result was God was with him, and success as king came with it.

Our children are watching everything we do from the good, the bad, and the ugly. Our prayer should always be that in the midst of it all that God shines through so that He can lead their ways as they grow up on their own.

Day 3

Heeding God's Word

2 Chronicles 18:1–7

Who doesn't like to hear things that are in their favor? It's nice to hear: "You will be successful"; "You will be victorious"; "You will be the best at what you do no matter what it is?" But what if you hear: "Destruction is upon you"; "You won't listen but you will fail if you go forward with your plan." It's harder to hear, and eventually, if all you hear is gloom and doom from them, you are not likely to call on him/her for advice anymore or at least be very hesitant.

That's what happened with Ahab, the king of Israel. Jehoshaphat had become an ally with Ahab due to marrying his daughter, and one day, Jehoshaphat went to see him. While there, Ahab asked if he would join him in fighting against Ramoth Gilead. Jehoshaphat, being wise in counsel, said, "We will join you in war but first seek the counsel of the Lord" (2 Chronicles 18:3–4). Ahab did everything but that. He asked four hundred prophets to come see him, and they all said, "Go, for God will give it into the king's hand" (18:6). I find it extremely interesting that there were four hundred "yes" men in the room all saying that God would give them the victory and Jehoshaphat was so close with God that he knew that none of them spoke from the Lord. Truth is the standard by which all things are measured, and if the truth doesn't line up with God, then it's not the truth. Plain and simple. However, how did he know? After all, they said, "God will give the victory into Ahab's hand." If your relationship with God is tight, then you just know.

"Jehoshaphat asked, 'Is there not a prophet of the Lord here whom we can inquire of?' The king answered, 'There is still one man through whom we can inquire of the Lord, but I hate him because he never prophesies anything good about me, but always bad. He is Micaiah, the son of Imiah'" (18:6–7). Ahab only wanted to hear the good that came his way. He knew that if Micaiah came, it would lead to bad news, so he decided not to ask until his back was to the wall. He knew that Jehoshaphat would not go into battle unless the Word of the Lord was spoken. How close are you to God that you would know truth over false teaching? We all want to say that it would be easy to tell them apart, but we have people preaching the word daily that claim to be preachers of God's Word when they are ticklers of your ear and telling you only things that you want to hear. In the end, if you follow the ways of the false teachers/prophets, it will lead to destruction, and you won't see it coming because you didn't take the time to listen nor did you have the desire to hear the hard truth over the lies.

It's important in our daily decisions to seek God's counsel whether we like what we hear or not because ultimately His Truth will be the only thing left standing. Will we be standing with Him or fall with the false prophets/teachers? Don't get sucked into the ways of the world—it will only lead to destruction.

Day 4

Heeding the Warning Signs

2 Chronicles 18:8–34

"Is there not a prophet of the Lord here whom we can inquire of?" Ahab had asked advice of four hundred prophets, but none of them were of the Lord. Jehoshaphat knew that and asked about it. Ahab intentionally left out Micaiah, the prophet, because he knew that he would hear what he didn't want to hear…the truth. Every time he asked Micaiah what the Lord said, it was always bad news for him, and he didn't want to hear it. So he said, "There is still one man through whom we can inquire of the Lord but I hate him because he never prophesies anything good about me, but always bad" (18:7). Jehoshaphat scolded him and said he shouldn't speak about God's man like that, and because of that, the king called Micaiah to come share what the Lord had told him.

I find it interesting that Micaiah repeated what the other prophets were saying, and even though the king had heard it four hundred times by the other prophets, he had a hard time believing him. He said, "How many times must I make you swear to me nothing but the truth in the name of the Lord?" (18:15). He knew that the others were ear ticklers, but Micaiah was a straight shooter and only told the truth. So, here's the question: who do you listen to? Do you desire the truth, or do you just want to hear what you want to hear? We all want to hear the good over the bad, but sometimes, knowing the bad can save your life if you listen to the warnings.

In March 2020, my husband had a heart attack at age forty-nine. In my opinion, he is too young for a heart attack, and frankly, I'm too young to be a widow, so thankfully, he was smart enough to heed the warnings. He had four episodes, and after the second, he was finally convinced to go to the ER. Blood work proved that he was having heart issues, and they did a heart catheterization to show the 95% blockage in his artery. They immediately put in a stint, and within two hours, he was back in his room to recover. What would've happened had he not listened to the advice of others? Nothing good, I can tell you that. But God is faithful to put the right people in place at the right time.

God was trying to do that with Ahab, but Ahab was hardheaded. Micaiah straight out said, "I saw the Lord and He said, 'Who will entice Ahab into attacking Ramoth Gilead and going to his death there?'" (18:19). A deceiving spirit stepped up and volunteered. God said, "You will succeed in enticing him. Go and do it" (18:21). God knew the heart of Ahab was not with God and He allowed the deceiving spirit to have control.

Do you know the difference between truth and deception? If so, are you willing to heed the warnings? If you are like my husband, heeding the warnings saved his life. If you are like Ahab, heeding the warnings will prove not to be as successful as we will see next. God puts circumstances, people, and Scripture in our paths for a reason. Be so connected to Him that when He shows you something, you are quick to listen.

Day 5

Deceptive Hearts

I was going to move on to more of the story but my thoughts went back to the verse when one of the spirits volunteered freely to go into prophets to give Ahab false information.

"God said, "Who will entice Ahab to attack Ramoth-Gilead and go to his death there?"

A spirit came forward and said, "I will entice him."

"By what means?" the Lord asked.

"I will go be a lying spirit in the mouths of the prophets of yours."

The Lord said, "You will have success, go and do it" (18:19–21).

So, as I read that portion of scripture, it reminded of this crazy Coronavirus. Our world has gotten so out of hand over the years/decades/centuries, that we will believe anything that comes our way *besides* the Lord.

We hear the media say there is a pandemic, and everyone rushes to the stores for toilet paper, cleaning supplies, hand sanitizer, milk, and bread. The leader says shut down everything from schools to churches and stay six feet apart from everyone and the followers that this world has become, say "okay," *without* a thought of going to God first. This world needs a priority check. If we don't come back to listening to God first, then we will all die from the most random of things. We must seek God's direction in all we do.

Back to the story, Micaiah said to Ahab, "So now the Lord has put a lying spirit in the mouths of these prophets of yours. The Lord has decreed disaster for you" (18:22). Zedekiah, one of the prophets came up and slapped Micaiah for the words spoken. Ahab got so angry that he said, "Put this fellow in prison and give him nothing but bread and water until I return safely." Micaiah said, "If you ever return safely, then the Lord has not spoken through me. Mark my words, all you people!" (18:26–27). The rest of the story will come tomorrow.

Our world is so quick to jump on any bandwagon that comes our way except listening to God. And He is the only one who can offer peace in the midst of trials and chaos. We must heed the Truth over lies. We must continue to meet together and worship Him. He is our life force. He is our Rock. He is the only way through, and He will be with you every step of the way.

Day 6

You Can't Run from God

After Micaiah was put in prison, Ahab and Jehoshaphat went up to Ramoth-Gilead. One thing I have noticed that after Micaiah told the truth, Jehoshaphat has been completely silent. He went with Ahab knowing what was prophesied was disaster. I don't know if he went along to protect Ahab or had strong convictions about attacking Ramoth-Gilead, or he wanted to be a spectator to see the destruction, but we do know that he went.

Ahab thought he could run from the prophecy set before him, so he said to Jehoshaphat, "'I will enter the battle in disguise, but you wear your royal robes.' So, the king went into battle in disguise" (18:29).

> "Now the king of Aram had ordered his chariot commanders, 'Do not fight with anyone, small or great, except the king of Israel.' When the chariot commanders saw Jehoshaphat, they thought, 'This is the king of Israel.' So, they turned to attack him, but Jehoshaphat cried out, and the Lord helped him. God drew them away from him, for when the chariot commanders saw that he was not the king of Israel, they stopped pursuing him."

> But someone drew his bow at random and hit the king of Israel between the sections of his armor. The king told the chariot driver, "Wheel around and get me out of the fighting. I've been wounded." All day long the battle raged, and the king of Israel propped himself up in his chariot facing the Arameans until evening. Then at sunset he died" (18:30–34).

Try as we might to change what has already been laid out for our lives, God already knows the twists and turns we will take to get to our final destination. He has His eyes set on us at all times. There is no place we can go that God is not already there.

My husband was reading a book by Viktor Frankel, and it talked about how death came to see a man to tell him he was going to die. The man asked for the fastest horse, so he could run away to Tehran without being caught by death, and he would live. Death came back and said, "Where is this man?" And they told him that he ran away on the fastest horse so that death would not get him. The man asked death, "Where are you headed?" And death said, "Tehran."

The point is that God knows when you are born and when you will die. He also knows the choices you will make in between. Some of those choices will be good, and some will be bad. Some of those choices will be led by God's guidance and others by your own choosing. But God is the only one that knows the end result. We cannot hide from God. Ultimately, we have to choose: who will you follow? God or yourself? If you are smart, your choice will always be God. Choose wisely.

Day 7

Judge Wisely

When Jehoshaphat came back from battle, Jehu, the seer, had some words of warning for him. "Should you help the wicked and love those who hate the Lord? Because of this, the wrath of the Lord is upon you. There is however, some good left in you for you have rid the land of the Asherah poles and have set your heart on seeking God" (19:2–3). Jehoshaphat just went to battle with Ahab who strictly went against the warnings of God, and he survived. Even though he had heard the warnings, he too chose alongside Ahab to go to battle. With the warning, that might've put a little bit more fear of God back into his life because after the conversation with Jehu, he went out to make his country right again in the sight of the Lord.

Jehoshaphat appointed judges to help fortify the cities and turn them back to the Lord and appointed some Levites "to administer the law of the Lord and to settle disputes" (19:8). He gave words of warning to both the judges and Levites:

a. "Consider carefully what you do because you aren't judging for man and but for the Lord" (19:6).
b. "You must serve faithfully and wholeheartedly in the fear of the Lord. Whatever situation comes your way, you are to warn them not to sin against the Lord, otherwise His wrath will come on you and your brothers. Do this and you will not sin" (19:9–10).

We are so flippant in our decisions these days because we see the lack of consequences that come our way when we go against the Lord. We think we are invincible, but God sees all, and He waits to see if we will turn back to Him, knowing all along what the result will be. Jehoshaphat, even though He knew it was wrong, went to battle with Ahab, and Jehu found him later to let him know in any uncertain terms, God knew what he had done and wasn't happy. That was his wake-up call. It was a time of decision, and he chose to restore his country. His father, Asa, when reprimanded chose anger and bitterness, and in five years, he was brought to his demise. Jehoshaphat chose the Lord, and his reign flourished. He set people in places that would give proper direction and guidance and then encouraged them all: "Act with courage, and may the Lord be with those who do well" (19:11b).

And so, I say to you in these challenging times, act with courage and may the Lord be with you as you do well. Choose wisely. Choose the Lord always over anything else.

Day 8

God Is Faithful

There is a song that keeps replaying in my head every morning when I get up—a song of comfort in the midst of chaos. It's called "Never Once" by Jason Ingram, Matt Redmon, and Tim Wanstall. These lyrics are:

> "Standing on this mountaintop, looking just how far we've come,
> Knowing that for ev'ry step You were with us.
> Kneeling on this battleground, seeing just how much You've done,
> Knowing ev'ry victory was Your pow'r in us.
> Scars and struggles on the way, but with joy our hearts can say,
> Yes, our hearts can say:
>
> Never once did we ever walk alone. Never once did you leave us on our own.
> You are faithful. God, You are faithful. You are faithful. God, You are faithful.
>
> Ev'ry step we are breathing in Your grace.
> Evermore we'll be breathing in your praise.

You are faithful. God, You are faithful. You are faithful. God, You are faithful."

Our time on this earth is uncertain, and in today's time of media madness of gloom and doom, it is even more certain. Jehoshaphat was having one of those gloom and doom moments in his reign. "He was being so faithful to the Lord's guidance that some of the other countries (the Moabites and Meunites) came to make war" (2 Chronicles 20:1). Jehoshaphat's men came to him and said, "A vast army is coming against you from Edom from the other side of the sea and they have already reached Hazazon Tamar. Jehoshaphat was alarmed but resolved to inquire of the Lord, and he proclaimed a fast for all Judah. The people came from every town to seek help from the Lord" (2 Chronicles 20:2–3). Jehoshaphat began to pray in front of the people to the Lord regarding their need for His help.

His prayer to God is so fitting to today. Here is what he prayed: "O Lord, God of our fathers, are you not the God who is in heaven? You rule over all the kingdoms of the nations. Power and might are in your hand and no one can withstand you. O our God, did you not drive out the inhabitants of this land before your people Israel and give it forever to the descendants of Abraham, your friend? They have lived in it and built in it a sanctuary for Your Name, saying, if calamity comes upon us, whether the sword of judgment, or plague or famine, we will stand in your presence before this temple that bears Your Name and will cry out to you in our distress, and You will hear us and save us" (20:6–9).

But now we have this virus that is spreading so quickly around the world and the fear of the unknown has spread even faster. "We have no power to face this vast army (unknown fears/future) that is attacking us. We do not know what to do, but our eyes are on You" (20:12).

After Jehoshaphat finished praying, while everyone in Judah stood with him, the Spirit of the Lord came upon Jehaziel. He said, "Listen! This is what the Lord says to you: Do not be afraid or discouraged. For the battle is not yours, but God's. You will not have to fight this battle. Take up your positions; stand firm and see the deliverance the Lord will give you. Do not be afraid; do not be discouraged. Go out and face them tomorrow and the Lord will be with you. Listen! Have faith in the Lord your God and you will be upheld. Have faith in His leaders (prophets) and you will be successful" (2 Chronicles 20:15–18, 20).

In the midst of it all, he and the people began to sing, "Give thanks to the Lord, for His love endures forever" (2 Chronicles 20:21). As they sang, God set traps and ambushes for the armies coming against them. By the time Jehoshaphat and his men got to the place where they were to battle, all they saw were dead bodies. God had gone before them and fought the battle for them just as He said He would do. God is faithful to do His part, but we too have to be faithful to do our part. We have to recognize that we have no power against the enemy but God does. All we have to do is "call on Him, seek His face, turn from our wicked ways and then He will heal our land" (2 Chronicles 7:14). The enemy may have a different face than back then, but the evil is still the same.

God calls us not to be afraid. He calls us to stand firm and see the deliverance of the Lord. He calls us to be faithful.

Day 9

It's Easy to Slide Back

After their victory over their enemies, they brought back all the spoils of war. There was so much that it took four days to gather it all. They returned joyfully to Jerusalem. "The fear of God came upon all the kingdoms of the countries when they heard how the Lord had fought against the enemies of Israel. And the kingdom of Jehoshaphat was at peace, for his God had given him rest on every side" (2 Chronicles 20:29–30). Peace in the midst of the storm.

Jehoshaphat reigned for twenty-five years until he was sixty years old, and he did well during that time. However, there was one thing he didn't get rid of, and that was the high places where the people could worship other gods. Even though Jehoshaphat was faithful to the Lord, "The people still had not set their hearts on the God of their fathers" (2 Chronicles 20:33).

I remember when I was losing massive amounts of weight after my youngest son was born and I was completely out of the largest size of clothes I had, I took two huge, full garbage bags, and threw all the clothes into the trash, never to be seen again. I received a lot of backlash for throwing away clothes, and after the initial purging, I began to give the rest away, but that's not the point. The point is that I had to completely clean my life out of the old past, so I wouldn't go back to it (ever). I have had totes of all different sizes of clothes in my basement before, and I would say, "I'll get in this size one day." But the key is to remove all that hinders you, throw it away, burn it, whatever, so that it is not a part of your life at all lurking in the background. Thankfully, I have never gone back to that size, and I never plan on it because it was a miserable place for me to be.

Jehoshaphat didn't do that. He kept the high places, and because of that, it became easy for his people to slip back into old ways when they got comfortable with being protected. I have noticed when I get lax in my studies and prayers, it is because everything is going so good. But when things get bad, my studies and prayers ramp up. That shouldn't happen. We should always be in training for what's to come. Be ready for battle. Our guard should be up, and we should be vigilant to walk in the ways of the Lord always.

We are called to obey.

Once You PURSUE, You Must OBEY, then You Need to ***LIVE***!

(Life In Various Experiences) Study of Psalm 119 (NIV)

Book Three

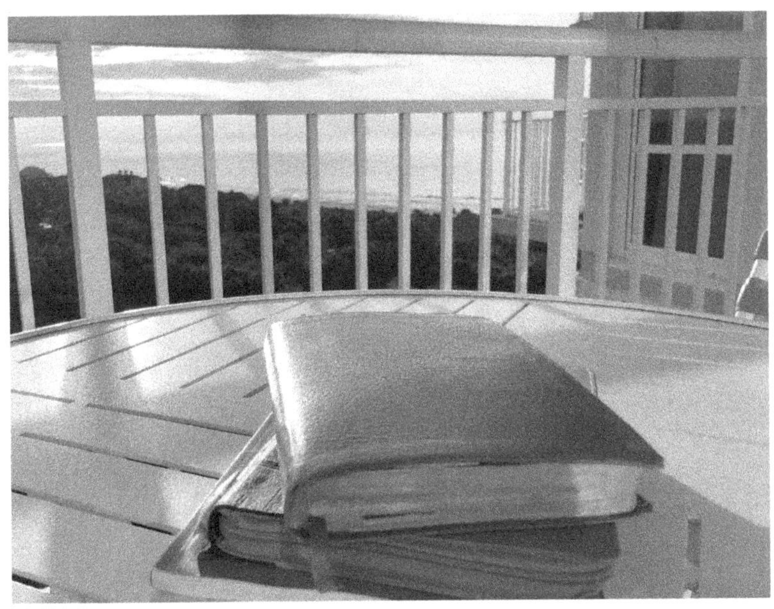

This Photo by Ann L. Knopp is licensed under CC BY-NC

Table of Contents

Introduction

Welcome to book 3 of the *Pursuing God Series*! When I started writing in 2017, I never thought it would turn into a three-book series. But it all fit so nicely together and flowed so easily. In book 1, we studied how Purposefully Understanding our Risen Savior Until Eternity (PURSUE), which led me to the question, "What then?" So my brain started tumbling over what happens when you pursue something and what you do once the pursuit reaches its destination. When it comes to pursuing God, there are only two choices: obey God or don't obey God. As I began to think of how to put obey into an acronym like PURSUE, it became an outline for book 2. We have Obedient believers, Bad decision makers, Evidence of obedience and You—are you obedient or not (OBEY). Once the outline came, so did the Bible characters that we would study. Jehoshaphat became my favorite character, and I even made 2 Chronicles 20:20 my verse for the year 2020 because his life so resonated in mine and it has been a foundation for many struggles through this year.

Now we are in book 3! I was out walking with a friend, and we were knocking around ideas of how this book series needed closure. First, we *pursue*. Then once we *pursue*, we must *obey*. What then? I think the word *live* hit us both at the same time, but it didn't have direction until I sat down to study Psalm 119. The longest chapter in the Bible is all about living your life through God's Word no matter what circumstance you are facing. Then LIVE came to life (Life in Various Experiences).

As I studied, the scripture seemed to just pop out into lists. The more I read Psalm 119, the more excited I became to share all I learned, so it just made sense that after we studied about the different characters of the Bible, we needed to apply the wisdom and *live* it out.

I do hope that you enjoy this study as much as I did and you are able to live out your pursuit and obedience to God daily.

"And this is His command: to believe in the name of His Son, Jesus Christ, and to love one another as He commanded us. Those who obey his commands live in Him and He in them. And this is how we know that He lives in us. We know it by the Spirit He gave us" (1 John 3:23–24).

Be blessed!

Day 1

Psalm 119:1–8

Blessed are those whose ways are blameless,
who walk according to the law of the Lord.
Blessed are those who keep his statutes
and seek him with all their heart—
they do no wrong
but follow his ways.
You have laid down precepts
that are to be fully obeyed.
Oh, that my ways were steadfast
in obeying your decrees!
Then I would not be put to shame
when I consider all your commands.
I will praise you with an upright heart
as I learn your righteous laws.
I will obey your decrees;
do not utterly forsake me.

Questions of the day:

1. Who is blessed according to the above scripture?

    a. Those whose ways are blameless.
    b. Those who walk according to the law.
    c. Those who keep His statutes.

d. Those who seek Him with all their heart (they do no wrong but follow His ways).

2. What happens when we obey His precepts (laws)?

a. Our ways are steadfast.
b. We are not put to shame.
c. We praise Him with an upright heart as we learn His righteous laws.
d. He does not forsake us!

> I always thank my God for you because of his grace given you in Christ Jesus. For in him you have been enriched in every way—with all kinds of speech and with all knowledge—God thus confirming our testimony about Christ among you. Therefore you do not lack any spiritual gift as you eagerly wait for our Lord Jesus Christ to be revealed. He will also keep you firm to the end, so that you will be blameless on the day of our Lord Jesus Christ. God is faithful, who has called you into fellowship with his Son, Jesus Christ our Lord. (1 Corinthians 1:4–9)

The scripture above adds depth to what the psalmist says about being blameless because God's grace is given in Christ; therefore, we have:

1. Been enriched in every way—in all our speaking and knowledge—because Christ is confirmed in us
2. No lack in spiritual gifts as we wait for the Lord to return or be revealed
3. Strength to the end, so that we will be blameless on the day He returns
4. God, who has called us into fellowship with Jesus, who is faithful.

When I see #3, there are days I just want to give up. But God is faithful (#4) to give me what I need (#2) to help me grow in all I do and say and think (#1) in order to have the strength (#3) to make it to the end still being faithful. I may not be perfect, but through Christ's blood, I am still found blameless. What a blessing!

As I look at the description of those that are blessed, I think about the Beatitudes that Jesus shared. Every beatitude started with "Blessed are" and then the description of each. The reason why they are blessed is because they each have an attitude toward loving God and serving others. Their walk with the Lord comes above everything else. They keep God's laws, and because they are so focused on Him, they are blessed with eternity in heaven, being comforted, filled with righteousness, mercy, the ability to see and hear from God, and be called sons and daughters of God.

God wants to bless us just as much as He wants us to glorify Him. It all comes from our attitude and what we choose to do with each decision we make daily. As the psalmist prays, "Oh that my ways were steadfast in obeying your decrees then I would not be put to shame when I consider all your commands" (v. 5–6). The more our attitude is focused on God and His Word, the more steadfast we become. The more steadfast we become, the less we will care about what the world thinks of us or throws our way. Then we can "praise Him with an upright heart" (v. 7), and as we continually learn His decrees, we can obey them to the fullest.

Day 2

Psalm 119:9–16

How can a young person stay on the path of purity?
By living according to your word.
I seek you with all my heart;
do not let me stray from your commands.
I have hidden your word in my heart
that I might not sin against you.
Praise be to you, Lord;
teach me your decrees.
With my lips I recount
all the laws that come from your mouth.
I rejoice in following your statutes
as one rejoices in great riches.
I meditate on your precepts
and consider your ways.
I delight in your decrees;
I will not neglect your word.

Question of the day:

How can a person stay pure or live on a path of purity?

1. Live according to His Word.
2. Seek Him with all your heart.
3. Hide His Word in your heart (memorize).

4. Pray for help not to stray (need God's help).
5. Be open to the Lord's teachings (be moldable).
6. Relive, recount what you are learning by sharing with others.
7. Worship and rejoice in the Lord in what you are discovering and learning.
8. Meditate on Scripture (think about it).
9. Consider your ways (confess your sins).
10. Delight in Scripture (crave it to the point that you don't neglect it).

We live in a world that is full of temptations. The temptations still hold to the same temptations that Satan tempted Eve with in the garden, but now they have become very in your face and blatant. Let's look back at Genesis 3 for a moment: "The serpent was more crafty than all the other wild animals God had made...when the woman saw that the fruit was good for food, pleasing to the eye and desirable for gaining wisdom, she took some and ate it" (3:1, 6). Satan is crafty, but he also knows what attracts you to things you shouldn't be doing or seeing or saying. Yet we succumb to these temptations time and time again.

I am a checklist kind of girl, and I need lists to keep me focused on getting things accomplished or help with my struggles. These verses are a perfect checklist to help on those troublesome, temptation-filled days. You may have temptations, but God supplies ways to get through the struggle. He may not take it away, but He becomes your strength to muscle through. You don't have to give in. God will provide a support system. God will give you the scripture you need at just the right moment. We have to be willing to learn His ways to follow them, confess our sins, then He will give us the longing we need for Him over the longings of this world. It may take time, but He is faithful to those who seek His face.

Day 3

Psalm 119:17–24

Be good to your servant while I live,
that I may obey your word.
Open my eyes that I may see
wonderful things in your law.
I am a stranger on earth;
do not hide your commands from me.
My soul is consumed with longing
for your laws at all times.
You rebuke the arrogant, who are accursed,
those who stray from your commands.
Remove from me their scorn and contempt,
for I keep your statutes.
Though rulers sit together and slander me,
your servant will meditate on your decrees.
Your statutes are my delight;
they are my counselors.

Question of the day:

What should my attitude be as I read Scripture?

1. Obedience to His Word.
2. Open eyes to see the wonderful things in Scripture.

3. Pray that His commands aren't hidden (or could be understood).
4. Long to be in Scripture every day.
5. Remove from me the negativity that surrounds me so that I can focus on Scripture.
6. Meditate on Scripture. Think about it, memorize it, use it in conversation.
7. Delight in Scripture, and let it be my counselor daily.

> I pray that the eyes of your heart may be enlightened in order that you may know the hope to which he has called you, the riches of his glorious inheritance in his holy people, and his incomparably great power for us who believe. That power is the same as the mighty strength he exerted when he raised Christ from the dead and seated him at his right hand in the heavenly realms, far above all rule and authority, power and dominion, and every name that is invoked, not only in the present age but also in the one to come. (Ephesians 1:18–21)

Based on Ephesians 1:18–21, where Paul prays for eyes to be opened, there are three things that he asks for us to be able to see:

1. You may know the hope to which He has called you.
2. You may know the riches of His glorious inheritance in the saints.
3. You may know His incomparably great power for us who believe.

What is that great power like?

"It is like the working of His might strength which He exerted in Christ when He raised Him from the dead and seated Him at His right hand in the heavenly realms far above all rule and authority, power and dominion, and every title that can be given, not only in the present age but also in the one to come" (Ephesians 1:19b–21).

Attitude is everything. It shows if you are genuine or not. For instance, when the boys were fighting when they were younger, I would make them apologize to each other. They didn't want to, and you could cut the tension with a knife, but they would say through gritted teeth and a growl, "Sorry." Then I said, "Say it like you mean it." It would take a few trials and some "Aw, Mom, do we have tos?" to get them to be laughing and playing again, then the attitude of the house changed as soon as the attitude of the boys changed.

That is the same with our attitude toward reading scripture and incorporating it into our lives. We should be obedient to what it says because it is our guide for living. As we become obedient, then our eyes will become open to new things in scripture. I find new things in scripture all the time—it's like treasure hunting in an open field. God doesn't hide his treasures from you, but you might have to look beyond your place in the field to find it. As His Word is revealed, you will hunger for more and long to have your quiet time every day. As you hunger, you find that you want to block out the negativity of the world so you can focus and meditate on His Word. Then it will become your delight, and no matter the situation, the counsel of scripture will be able to guide you.

Psalm 119:17–24 is not only a list of what your attitude should be toward scripture, but also it's a flowchart, and it all starts with obedience. Once your heart obeys God's Word, the rest of you will follow. I've said this before, but it still holds true in this instance as well, "Actions must lead your feelings." If you let your feelings guide your life, you would never get out of bed in the morning. It's important to do what you know is right to do, and then everything else will fall into place.

As you obey, your list of what God has called you to be and to do will continually get longer because your eyes will be opened to more of His activity in the world. And that's okay because the more God shows you, your delight in Him will become that much greater.

What is God showing you today?

Day 4

Psalm 119:25–32

I am laid low in the dust;
preserve my life according to your word.
I gave an account of my ways and you answered me;
teach me your decrees.
Cause me to understand the way of your precepts,
that I may meditate on your wonderful deeds.
My soul is weary with sorrow;
strengthen me according to your word.
Keep me from deceitful ways;
be gracious to me and teach me your law.
I have chosen the way of faithfulness;
I have set my heart on your laws.
I hold fast to your statutes, Lord;
do not let me be put to shame.
I run in the path of your commands,
for you have broadened my understanding.

Question of the day:

What to pray as the Scripture becomes a part of you?

1. Forgiveness—give an account, save our life
2. Understanding—of what is read so we can meditate on it and use it

3. Strength—in knowledge and life
4. Protection
5. Grace
6. Choose to be faithful and hold fast to our commitment

> For the word of God is alive and active. Sharper than any double-edged sword, it penetrates even to dividing soul and spirit, joints and marrow; it judges the thoughts and attitudes of the heart. Nothing in all creation is hidden from God's sight. Everything is uncovered and laid bare before the eyes of him to whom we must give account. (Hebrews 4:12–13)

Based on Hebrews 4:12–13, what is the truth and power of God's Word based on?

1. It's living and active.
2. It is so sharp; it penetrates straight to the soul.
3. It judges thoughts and attitudes of the heart.
4. Nothing is hidden from God's sight.
5. Everything is laid before God when we have to one day give an account for our lives.

So because of that, I choose to be faithful. I choose to hold fast to His statutes. I choose to run in God's direction of understanding (Psalm 119:30–32).

The Bible is full of prayers that you can use in your own prayer life. Jesus was asked by the disciples to teach them to pray, and so he taught them "The Lord's Prayer" as we call it. This gives you every aspect of prayer from praise, adoration, confession, to asking for yourself and others. As prayer becomes a part of who you are and you go deeper into your prayer life, instead of just praying for the surface of things, you can become more specific which is where David was getting to in his life. Psalm 119:25–32 helps find those specifics: forgiveness, understanding, strength, protection, grace, and faithfulness.

God didn't give us His Word just to read. He gave us His Word to use. He gave it to us as an instruction manual. He gave us Jesus as the manual's teacher and guide. He quoted scripture in His life, and therefore, we should use His words as well in conversation and prayer. There is nothing on this earth that hasn't already been seen by God; there is nothing that surprises him. There is nothing new to pray; however, we are to pray. It is our communication with God, and if we stop talking long enough to listen, He may just reveal His heart to you whether it is in scripture or thought or through someone else. As it says at the end of verse 32, God had "broadened his horizons through understanding because scripture had become a part of him." Therefore, when he prayed, scripture came flowing out of him.

Our lives need to be so immersed in God's Word that when we pray, His words come rolling out of us. His Word is active and living, and it penetrates to the soul, so when it becomes a part of your life, it becomes a part of your core. When it becomes a part of your core, then what you pray becomes more than "Thank you for this day, help me get through it."

Seize every opportunity to read His Word, and seek His face. You will be changed because of it.

Day 5

Psalm 119:33–40

Teach me, Lord, the way of your decrees,
that I may follow it to the end.
Give me understanding, so that I may keep your law
and obey it with all my heart.
Direct me in the path of your commands,
for there I find delight.
Turn my heart toward your statutes
and not toward selfish gain.
Turn my eyes away from worthless things;
preserve my life according to your word.
Fulfill your promise to your servant,
so that you may be feared.
Take away the disgrace I dread,
for your laws are good.
How I long for your precepts!
In your righteousness preserve my life.

Questions of the day:

What is God teaching me through Scripture?

1. Understanding—to keep God's Law and obey it with all my heart
2. Direction—where I find delight in His path

3. Turning to God not selfish gain
4. Turn eyes away from worthless things; preserve my life according to God's Word
5. Promises fulfilled so that God may be feared
6. Disgrace is removed because God's Law is good

In verse 33, it says "teach me Your ways." So what are God's ways? (Read John 14:1–10.)

1. Don't be troubled.
2. Trust in God and Jesus.
3. A place has been prepared for each of us who believe.
4. Jesus is the only way to get to Him.
5. Follow Jesus's examples of how to live.
6. We are image bearers so if we are to live in Christ, our mind needs to be like Christ.

When I think of God's ways versus my own, I often just come up with the simple question of "Why?" Then the verse in Isaiah 55:8 pops into my mind, "For my thoughts are not your thoughts, neither are your ways my ways. As the heavens are higher than earth so are my ways higher than your ways and my thoughts than your thoughts." And the answer to my question every time is, "because God loves me and you." He saw from the beginning to the end, the trials and triumphs, and made it all anyway. In the end, He wins. We are to trust in God alone.

This portion of the Psalm gives us a list of what happens when we turn to Scripture for our teaching of life. We receive understanding, direction, preservation of life, promises fulfilled, and disgrace is removed. This solidifies Proverbs 3:5–6. When we trust in the Lord with all who we are and we don't try to do all the explaining for a situation but rely on God's understanding, then He will direct us completely in the ways to go. Our job is to follow His leading. "Turning our hearts toward His law and not toward selfish gain" (Psalm 119:36) is essential when you follow His leading because in the end, it is God who should get the glory, not you. Trust is hard in an untrusting world, but God will never lead you astray.

Day 6

Psalm 119:41–48

May your unfailing love come to me, Lord,
your salvation, according to your promise;
then I can answer anyone who taunts me,
for I trust in your word.
Never take your word of truth from my mouth,
for I have put my hope in your laws.
I will always obey your law,
for ever and ever.
I will walk about in freedom,
for I have sought out your precepts.
I will speak of your statutes before kings
and will not be put to shame,
for I delight in your commands
because I love them.
I reach out for your commands, which I love,
that I may meditate on your decrees.

Question of the day:

What happens when God's unfailing love comes to me?

1. I can answer anyone who taunts me for I trust in God's Word.

2. Word of truth is in my mouth for I have put my hope in God's Law.
3. Obedience to God's Law
4. Walk in freedom
5. Speak of God's Law before leaders and not be put to shame.
6. Delight in God's commands because I love them.
7. Meditate on God's commands and decrees.

Boldness and *strength*—two words that come to mind when I think of the result of God's love coming to me. I receive a boldness to speak scripture and His truth in any situation no matter how intimidating or easy feeling it may seem. I remember when I was working at a local high school and we were just coming back from a wonderful summer away. It was time to get back to work. I had been so filled in my time with the Lord all summer that scripture kept flowing out in my conversations. Christians and non-Christians alike responded with such ease. Some didn't know I was quoting scripture and others that did spoke with scripture as well. It was fascinating to see God's love work so freely among His people. There truly was a freedom, and I took great delight in seeing it all unfold. Those conversations made me want to delve into scripture even more to see what else He could real in my life and all that surrounded me.

There is also a strength that comes when God's unfailing love becomes a part of me or you. Sometimes, speaking the truth is not the easiest thing to do. There may be times when confronted we have to speak against the crowd. It is in those times, God gives us strength beyond ourselves to be obedient to His calling.

When I think of situations like that, Stephen is the first one that pops into my mind. He was about to be stoned to death. He could've walked away from it all walked away from it all and said nothing, but his life was encompassed in God. God gave him the strength to speak boldly. He probably thought, *I'm going to die anyway, might as well go out swinging*. He preached an amazing sermon in Acts 7 and then was stoned to death. And guess who was holding the cloaks of the stoners—Saul. Saul would later become Paul who turned out to be the greatest missionary for the gospel. You never know what impact your words will make in a given situation. No one event in your life is unusable by God. That's why it's important to let God's Word become a part of you so His unfailing love will be able to do great things through you. And as He works, take notice and praise Him for it. He is worthy to be praised.

Day 7

Psalm 119:49–56

Remember your word to your servant,
for you have given me hope.
My comfort in my suffering is this:
Your promise preserves my life.
The arrogant mock me unmercifully,
but I do not turn from your law.
I remember, Lord, your ancient laws,
and I find comfort in them.
Indignation grips me because of the wicked,
who have forsaken your law.
Your decrees are the theme of my song
wherever I lodge.
In the night, Lord, I remember your name,
that I may keep your law.
This has been my practice:
I obey your precepts.

Question of the day:

How does the psalmist get through his times of darkness and "night?"

1. God's Word brings him hope.
2. God's promises preserve his life and bring comfort.

3. The arrogant mock but he stands strong and doesn't turn from God's Law.
4. Indignation grips him because of those that have forsaken God.
5. God's decrees are the theme of his song, and he remembers them through the night.

Darkness—whether it is literal where it is the middle of the night or virtual where it is a time of loneliness and hopelessness, both are often difficult to live through. More often than not, those two collide. You can't sleep at night, so you stare up into the blackness, and you begin to replay all your struggles. It makes for a long night when that happens.

However, there is hope. The psalmist had been through some really dark times in his life, and in his prayer of Psalm 119, he begins to pray hope through his darkness. Take a look back at the list of items that got him through his tough times. It starts with a glimmer of hope and through the steps of faith, trust, forgiveness, and grace. He is able to see past his darkness and focus on thanksgiving and a desire to learn more of God.

I remember when I had graduated from college and I had moved back home to figure out what I wanted to do with my life, Dad was pastoring a church in Maryville, Tennessee. They had a prayer room that was only a room with no connection to getting into the rest of the church. It was always open, and you could go in and pray anytime you wanted. I went a few times while I was at home, and every time I walked in, the burdens of the world weighed heavy on me; but when I walked out, there was a freedom and lightness to my step. My troubles were still there, but the prayer room wasn't about me and my troubles; it was about focusing on others and lifting up their needs to the Lord. The design of the room was a kneeling bench and a chair. The kneeling bench had a desk with a prayer book. The prayer book was filled with prayer requests, but it was also filled with answered prayers. It didn't just sit idle for years and never updated. You knew when prayers were answered and the effect it played on those praying for help. Once you were finished praying, then you added your own requests in the book and left them there knowing that God was mighty to save. He was merciful and gracious enough to answer.

I saw a picture one time on Facebook where it showed a small cat going in to pray and came out as a lion. That is what prayer does especially during dark times. God gives you the strength and power to walk through each day and not just make it through but to conquer the day with Him fighting the battles for you or with you.

Be encouraged today. You are not alone.

Day 8

Psalm 119:57–64

You are my portion, Lord;
I have promised to obey your words.
I have sought your face with all my heart;
be gracious to me according to your promise.
I have considered my ways
and have turned my steps to your statutes.
I will hasten and not delay
to obey your commands.
Though the wicked bind me with ropes,
I will not forget your law.
At midnight I rise to give you thanks
for your righteous laws.
I am a friend to all who fear you,
to all who follow your precepts.
The earth is filled with your love, Lord;
teach me your decrees.

Question of the day:

Because the Lord is our portion, what should be our commitment?

1. Obey His words.
2. Seek His face with all our heart.

3. Ask for grace.
4. Turn from our ways to God's ways.
5. Hasten to obey His commands.
6. Do not forget God's Law.
7. Give thanks and praise to God.
8. Be a friend to fellow believers.

I have heard a statement from people many times over the years which is, "I just wish God would lay out His plan for my life so I could follow it." or, "I'm just going to pray for God's will to be done." and then never make a decision. If you read the Bible with a desire to understand it, you will see God's heart for how He wants you to live your life.

It starts with the greatest of all commandments, "Love the Lord your God with all your heart, all your mind, all your soul and all your strength" (Mark 12:30 NIV). Then the second commandment is, "Love your neighbor as yourself" (Matthew 23:9 NIV). Those two commandments are broken down even further into the Ten Commandments in Exodus 20. If you want more, go to Micah 6:8 which says, "Act justly, love mercy, and walk humbly with your God." Even today's scripture gives you direction on how to follow God with your life. Obey Him. Seek Him. Ask for grace. Turn from your old ways. Don't forget God's Laws. Give thanks and praise to God. Be a friend.

Our Bible is a book full of instruction. We never have to question what God's will is for our lives. We were made to glorify and love Him with all our hearts and serve Him completely. As we do that, we love others in the name of Jesus so that we may be a light to bring others to Him. Simple? In concept, yes. But things of life seem to get in our way to where we put God on the back burner and put our fears in God's place. On those days, we need to get into His Word more. We need to have just a little more faith and trust that God is faithful and He will see us through.

God doesn't give instruction without His faithfulness to back up His promises. His promises run as rampant through scripture as

His instructions do. Through it all, God's faithfulness to His people reign supreme.

What is holding you back from fully following Him today?

Day 9

Psalm 119:65–72

Do good to your servant
according to your word, Lord.
Teach me knowledge and good judgment,
for I trust your commands.
Before I was afflicted I went astray,
but now I obey your word.
You are good, and what you do is good;
teach me your decrees.
Though the arrogant have smeared me with lies,
I keep your precepts with all my heart.
Their hearts are callous and unfeeling,
but I delight in your law.
It was good for me to be afflicted
so that I might learn your decrees.
The law from your mouth is more precious to me
than thousands of pieces of silver and gold.

Question of the day:

In verse 68, it says God is good, so how do we expand on that? (Read Psalm 86:5–15.)

1. God is forgiving.
2. God is good.

3. God is abounding in love to all who call on Him.
4. God listens to our cry for mercy.
5. God answers our call in times of trouble.
6. No one/Nothing can compare to God.
7. All nations will bring Him glory.
8. God is great.
9. God does marvelous deeds.
10. He alone is God.
11. God teaches us the way and the truth.
12. God gives us an undivided heart that we may fear His name.
13. God is greatly to be praised and glorified.
14. God's love is great toward me.
15. God delivers us from the fiery grave.
16. God is compassionate, gracious, abounding in love, slow to anger, abounding in love and faithfulness.

This set of scripture can also be broken down into a prayer.

> Lord, I love you! Teach me knowledge and good judgment for I trust in Your commands. You are good, and what You do is good; teach me Your decrees. Though the arrogant smear Christians with lies, I pray that You help me keep Your Word and delight in You as others hearts are growing callous. It is good for me to see this affliction because I know I need to learn so much more. You are worth far more than silver or gold. Amen!

The song "Good Father" came to mind when I read verse 68 about being a good God. Then my thoughts reverted to Jesus when He asked the rich young man, "Why do you ask me what is good? There is only One who is good. If you want to enter life, obey the commandments" (Matthew 19:17). The man proceeded to say, "I have kept all the commandments." Then Jesus said (because He knew the man's heart and he was a wealthy man), "Go and sell all you have, give it to the poor and come follow Me." The man was saddened and turned away because he knew the cost and he wasn't willing to make it. (Story found in Matthew 19:16-30)

While in quarantine, I have checked out social media, and there is one ad that makes me more annoyed than any other. I'm not going to tell you the company, but I will say it's a weight loss app. What annoys me about it is that they give you the success stories but don't share any insights with you on how they got there. They are hoping you will either trust them enough to buy into their plan sight unseen or be gullible enough to believe that these people actually used their product to get the body that is being advertised. I have even gotten to the checkout box several times because I got so desperate that day for any help I could find. Then a little voice says, "You know what you are supposed to do, just do it." And I cleared out my information and went about my day saving some money along the way.

When I read Psalm 86:5–15, there isn't anything hidden about God that will keep you from committing your life to Him. What He says, He will do. He is forgiving. He is loving. He does listen. He does answer. He does teach us. He does deliver us. And there is so much more! God is not an infomercial wanting your money only. God is God wanting *you*. When you commit your life to Him, you receive an abundance of blessings. You receive a gift that is not only received but allows you to give to others over and over again because God's love just grows and grows the more He lives and reigns within you.

"These instructions were given in keeping with the prophecies so that by following them you may fight the *good* fight, holding on to faith and a *good* conscience" (1 Timothy 1:18–19; italics mine). Today is a *good* day to come to the *good* Father and live in His *goodness*.

Day 10

Psalm 119:73–80

Your hands made me and formed me;
give me understanding to learn your commands.
May those who fear you rejoice when they see me,
for I have put my hope in your word.
I know, Lord, that your laws are righteous,
and that in faithfulness you have afflicted me.
May your unfailing love be my comfort,
according to your promise to your servant.
Let your compassion come to me that I may live,
for your law is my delight.
May the arrogant be put to shame for wronging me without cause;
but I will meditate on your precepts.
May those who fear you turn to me,
those who understand your statutes.
May I wholeheartedly follow your decrees,
that I may not be put to shame.

Question of the day:

What is God's involvement in my life?

1. His hands made me and formed me.
2. He gives me understanding to learn His commands.

3. He brings others into my life to rejoice that I have placed my hope in Him.
4. He created righteous laws.
5. He has given me unfailing love to be my comfort.
6. His compassion comes to me so I can live.
7. He puts the arrogant to shame.
8. He brings people my way so I can teach them about God's Word.

Psalm 139 further explores God's knowledge of the intricacies of my life.

1. He searches me and knows me.
2. He knows when I sit and when I rise.
3. He perceives my thoughts from afar.
4. He is familiar with my ways, knows when I go out and when I lie down.
5. He knows what I'm going to say before I say it.
6. He is behind and before me. There is nowhere I can go without Him being there too.
7. I can't hide in the darkness because He is light, and since He is always with me, even the darkest night will shine like the day.
8. He created me in my mother's womb, knit together every part of me.
9. He made my frame, and I am fearfully and wonderfully made.
10. All my days were written and ordained for me before I even came to be.
11. He searches me (again) because He knows my heart.
12. He tests me and knows my anxious thoughts.
13. He shows me my offensive ways.
14. Then He leads me in the everlasting way.

God sees me. From the beginning to the end, He sees me. God is involved in my life from the time I am conceived until eternity.

He placed me with my parents. He knew I would struggle with my weight. He knew who I would meet to marry (and when). He knew our children and the roads they would take. He knew the churches we would be a part of and the various jobs I would take. And in all of it, God said, "It is good."

I am thankful for the people He placed in my life along the way: ones that were friends and like-minded in Christ and those that God led me to minister to. Both are important, but in the end, the desire will always be that everyone will become like-minded in Christ.

His unfailing love never ceases. Because of that, I can know that I am never left alone. He is constantly guiding me. He turns me away from things I deem as important, and when I look back, I can see the path of destruction that it may lead to in the end. Where I don't always see where/why He's working, I know He is, and I am thankful.

"Even the darkest night will shine like the day for darkness is as day to You" (Psalm 139:12). That is a powerful statement: "your darkest night will shine like the day." The darkest day in history is when God had to turn His back on His Son because He couldn't look upon sin. And the sin that was placed on Jesus was so much from the past, present, and the future that God took His light away. We don't have to ever be afraid that God will not be with us. Jesus paid the ultimate sacrifice so that He would be by our side on the worst days of our lives. And on those worst days, with God's light shining, you can still see past the pain to a brighter future. God's light brings hope to a dark world. We don't walk in darkness because we have seen a great light and that light is Jesus. Live today with the hope of light in the darkness. Remember, when despair is at its greatest, God is there, and He will guide you through. Look up. Look out. Look around. Look past your spot. There's hope. Call out to Him today. He will answer you.

"Waymaker. Promise Keeper. Light in the dark world. My God, that is who You are!"

Day 11

Psalm 119:81–88

My soul faints with longing for your salvation,
but I have put my hope in your word.
My eyes fail, looking for your promise;
I say, "When will you comfort me?"
Though I am like a wineskin in the smoke,
I do not forget your decrees.
How long must your servant wait?
When will you punish my persecutors?
The arrogant dig pits to trap me,
contrary to your law.
All your commands are trustworthy;
help me, for I am being persecuted without cause.
They almost wiped me from the earth,
but I have not forsaken your precepts.
In your unfailing love preserve my life,
that I may obey the statutes of your mouth.

Question of the day:

What did the psalmist do during his times of distress?

Through whatever came his way, he clung to God's Word because it was his law, his guide, and his boundary.

Psalmist's Situation	Psalmist's Response
v. 81—My soul faints with longing for your salvation.	I have put my hope in Your word.
v. 82—When will you comfort me? v. 83—feel like a wineskin in smoke (useless, cracked, shriveled)	I do not forget your decrees.
v. 84—How long must I wait? When will you punish my persecutions? v. 85—The arrogant set traps for me.	v. 86—All your commands are trustworthy, help me?
v. 87—They almost wiped me out.	I have not forsaken your precepts. v. 88—Preserve my life with your unfailing love so that I may obey the statutes of your mouth.

When distress comes my way, I sometimes have to be shaken to get me back in my right way of thinking. That's why boundaries are so good because boundaries encompass me with truth. The truth of God's Word hems me in on every side so that when I bounce my distress off of it, it comes back to me with the promises of God. That's why sharing my heart no matter what it's about, with God is so important. Because once I get the distress off my mind and lay at the feet of Jesus, He can fill me with His promises of truth, love, and hope. That's why it's also important to memorize Scripture or at least know the gist. Because once you share your distress, He will fill you up with His Word to carry with you through the day.

David was an amazing example of sharing his heart, and then by the end of his prayer, he had come to terms with his situation, and all that was left was praising God for His faithfulness. God's Law is our boundary. God's Law keeps us going in the right direction. Share your heart with God—your whole heart. He knows your heart anyway but He wants you to acknowledge everything in your life so that He can fill you with all He wants to give you. But if you hold on to the distress, then you are left with an unopened gift of blessings for the day. Don't miss the blessing!

Day 12

Psalm 119:89–96

Your word, Lord, is eternal;
it stands firm in the heavens.
Your faithfulness continues through all generations;
you established the earth, and it endures.
Your laws endure to this day,
for all things serve you.
If your law had not been my delight,
I would have perished in my affliction.
I will never forget your precepts,
for by them you have preserved my life.
Save me, for I am yours;
I have sought out your precepts.
The wicked are waiting to destroy me,
but I will ponder your statutes.
To all perfection I see a limit,
but your commands are boundless.

Question of the day:

How does the psalmist exalt the faithfulness of God?

1. God's Word is eternal.
2. God's faithfulness endures through all generations.
3. God established the earth, and it endures.

4. God's law endures until today for all who serve Him.
5. If God's Law had not been his delight, He would've perished.
6. God preserved life through His precepts.
7. God's commands have no limits (boundless).

Our response to His faithfulness: (Psalm 100)

(This is the response of those who understand and embrace His truths.)

1. Shout for joy to the Lord.
2. Worship the Lord with gladness.
3. Come before Him with joyful songs.
4. Know that the Lord is God.
5. It is He who made us and we are His people.
6. Enter His gates with thanksgiving (give thanks) and His courts with praise (praise His name).
7. The Lord is good, and His love endures forever.
8. His faithfulness continues through all generations.

How do we worship? Worship is our time to give back to the One that gave everything for us. Every person worships differently. Some are very extravagant in their worship and put on a show for all to see. Others are very quiet and reserved and want no attention. Then there are those in the middle. But God's desire, no matter the way expressed, is to have a heart that is genuine. If your heart isn't genuine, then the worship isn't real, and God isn't glorified—you are. When you think back to Cain and Abel, they both came to offer their sacrifices, but only one truly worshipped Him, and God knew it.

God wants your genuine worship. Sing His praises. Meditate on His Word. Give Him thanks, and praise for all He has done and will do in the future. Serve Him. Love others with God's love in you. Always keep in mind that God is faithful and His love endures forever. Let Him lead you daily.

Day 13

Psalm 110:97–104

Oh, how I love your law!
I meditate on it all day long.
Your commands are always with me
and make me wiser than my enemies.
I have more insight than all my teachers,
for I meditate on your statutes.
I have more understanding than the elders,
for I obey your precepts.
I have kept my feet from every evil path
so that I might obey your word.
I have not departed from your laws,
for you yourself have taught me.
How sweet are your words to my taste,
sweeter than honey to my mouth!
I gain understanding from your precepts;
therefore, I hate every wrong path.

Question of the day:

What are the benefits to meditating on God's Word?

1. His commands are always with me.
2. His words make me wiser than my enemies.
3. I have more insight than all my teachers.

4. I have more understanding than my elders because I obey God's precepts.
5. I have kept my feet from every evil path so that I might obey Your Word.
6. I have not departed from God's Laws because He has taught me.
7. God's Word is sweeter than honey—I crave it.
8. I gain understanding from His precepts; therefore, I know the wrong path and hate going down it.

God's Word is sure and steadfast. If it is a part of who you are, then it becomes your foundation for every step and every decision. Fear cannot lead where God is in control. I teach on keeping God's Word in your heart and mind for specific struggling times. We don't always carry around a Bible, but we can carry what He says in our minds. The more you study, the more you memorize; the more you put His Word first in conversation, the easier it is to live His Word daily.

When I have been in conversation before and scripture pops into my mind that relates to the conversation, I don't say, "In such and such chapter of such and such" because that will often ruin the flow (especially if it's not with a Christian). I simply quote what the scripture says. Now if they ask where the wisdom came from, then I am quick to share, and God does amazing things through that. Now if you are talking with a Christian, chapter and verse may be relevant to the conversation. But if you are meditating on His Word, He will give you understanding and wisdom to use His words with other people.

When you meditate on His Word, you crave it and can't get enough of it. I challenge you to start taking a verse a day and keep it with you. Whether it be on a card or in your mind and then watch what God does with your conversations and who He leads you to talk with. Not only will you be strengthened in your insight into God's Word, but it might just change the lives of those around you.

Day 14

Psalm 119:105–112

Your word is a lamp for my feet,
a light on my path.
I have taken an oath and confirmed it,
that I will follow your righteous laws.
I have suffered much;
preserve my life, Lord, according to your word.
Accept, Lord, the willing praise of my mouth,
and teach me your laws.
Though I constantly take my life in my hands,
I will not forget your law.
The wicked have set a snare for me,
but I have not strayed from your precepts.
Your statutes are my heritage forever;
they are the joy of my heart.
My heart is set on keeping your decrees
to the very end.

Question of the day:

What does God's light do in your daily walk?

1. His Word is a lamp for my feet.
2. His Word is a light for my path.
3. His Word helps me follow His righteous laws.

4. His Word helps me see through the suffering to who can help.
5. In the darkness, enemies set snares for traps, but because I walk in God's light, He allows me to see the traps before I walk in them.

> I am the light of the world. Whoever follows me will never walk in darkness, but will have the light of life. (John 8:12)

I read a book called *Just Enough Light for the Step I'm On* by Stormie O'Martian. The premise of the book has stuck with me for longer than twenty years. Sometimes, we want to see the full picture of what God is doing in our lives, but if we did, we might be too afraid to continue. Why? Because it may seem insurmountable at the time and you aren't ready *yet* for what is to come. So, as it says in Psalm 119:105, "God gives you a lamp for your feet" (which is light enough for each step you take) "and a light for your path" (which is enough light to see things lurking around you).

Satan loves working in the darkness because he loves setting traps to make you falter. The key is to use God's light to bring the traps to light. Once they are seen, then they can be avoided. Jesus is the Light. He shines brightly in the darkness to where it's like the noonday sun. He also continually walks beside you to put out the dangers that you may be oblivious to walking by yourself.

In God's wisdom of you and your future, He knows exactly how much light to shine your way. He may give you just enough light for each step, or He may light everything so you can see it all. Either way, He is the one that shines the light. He is the one that knows how much you can handle in any given situation. He is the one that protects you from the enemy's snares. He is the one that walks beside you day by day. He is the One. Let Him be your guide today.

Day 15

Psalm 119:113–120

I hate double-minded people,
but I love your law.
You are my refuge and my shield;
I have put my hope in your word.
Away from me, you evildoers,
that I may keep the commands of my God!
Sustain me, my God, according to your promise, and I will live;
do not let my hopes be dashed.
Uphold me, and I will be delivered;
I will always have regard for your decrees.
You reject all who stray from your decrees,
for their delusions come to nothing.
All the wicked of the earth you discard like dross;
therefore I love your statutes.
My flesh trembles in fear of you;
I stand in awe of your laws.

Question of the day:

How can we put our hope in His Word?

Faith. Plain and simple. He sustains and upholds me. Why? Because of His promises, therefore, I have hope and He has become my refuge and my shield.

How can God provide protection for His children?

1. The Lord is my strength.
2. He is my deliverer.
3. He is my rock in whom I take refuge.
4. He is my shield of victory and horn of my salvation.
5. He saves me from enemies, defeats them.
6. He hears me when I cry for help and comes.
7. He is perfect and flawless.
8. He makes my feet to stand on the heights.
9. He trains my hands for battle.
10. He is worthy to be praised!

"Why so downcast, O my soul, put your trust in Him. Put your trust in Him. Put your trust in Him." That little praise song keeps rolling around in my head as I read today's scripture. God has continually shown Himself to be faithful time and time again, and we continue to worry: worry about the future, worry about this or that. And all it does is zap our time away from the present, the moments that He has placed us in to enjoy.

Psalm 119:114 says, "You are my refuge and my shield; I have put my hope in Your word." Why put your hope in a God you haven't seen? Because His promises are true. His Word is true. What He says He will do, He has done and continues to do. Even in the bad times, He is working in it for His good. There is so much good that has come out of the quarantine: families are together, pollution is down, people are showing their faith more, we are learning new avenues to share God's Word, etc. Of course, the bad is always going to be around, but God will bring us through victoriously. He will defeat the enemy. During this time, He is training us for battle. Are you ready? Faith, trust, and hope are needed, and He will provide. You just have to ask for it, and He will strengthen you, shield you, and deliver you.

Day 16

Psalm 119:121–128

I have done what is righteous and just;
do not leave me to my oppressors.
Ensure your servant's well-being;
do not let the arrogant oppress me.
My eyes fail, looking for your salvation,
looking for your righteous promise.
Deal with your servant according to your love
and teach me your decrees.
I am your servant; give me discernment
that I may understand your statutes.
It is time for you to act, Lord;
your law is being broken.
Because I love your commands
more than gold, more than pure gold,
and because I consider all your precepts right,
I hate every wrong path.

Question of the day:

How is having discernment and wisdom beneficial to your walk with the Lord?

1. Do what is righteous and just.
2. Ensure your well-being.

3. Be easily taught.
4. Understand God's Laws and follow them.
5. Consider all God's precepts as right and follow them (treasure it).

Proverbs 2—"The Lord gives wisdom" (v. 6).

1. From God's mouth come knowledge and understanding.
2. He holds victory in store for the upright.
3. He is a shield to those whose walk is blameless.
4. He guards the course of the just.
5. He protects the way of His faithful ones.

Then (once you receive His wisdom):

1. You will understand what is right, just, and fair (and every good path).
2. Wisdom will enter your heart.
3. Knowledge will be pleasant to your soul.
4. Discretion will protect you.
5. Understanding will guard you.
6. Wisdom will save you from the ways of wicked men.
7. Wisdom will save you from leaving the straight paths to walk in dark ways.
8. Wisdom will save you from delighting in wrong and rejoicing in the perverseness of evil.
9. Wisdom will save you from adulterousness.
10. Wisdom will lead you in the ways of good men.
11. Wisdom will keep you on the paths of righteousness.

This world is so full of temptations and small tweaks from the truth that we don't often see when the truth evolves into a lie. And by the time you realize it, it's too late, and you're stuck. It's exactly like a frog in a pot. If you put a frog in boiling water, he'll jump right out. But if you put a frog in room temperature water and slowly turn up the heat, he'll never notice the change because he becomes comfortable in his surroundings to the point that he never leaves the pot when it gets too hot.

Wisdom and discernment allow you to see even the small tweaks from truth and avenues to steer clear of the temptations that lurk in every corner. The only way to truly be able to discern right from wrong *and* have strength enough to walk away from the temptation is to be in God's Word. Let God engulf you so that He can fill you with His truth. He is strong enough to carry you through it all. He is your shield, your guard, your protection, and your victory. But without Him, "the wicked will be cut off from the land and the unfaithful will be torn from it" (Proverbs 2:22).

For me, I desire knowledge and understanding so that I can know that even in the smallest tweaks from the truth; I can see it and not walk in it. It's happening all around us every day. "Be self-controlled and alert. The devil prowls around like a roaring lion looking for someone to devour. Resist him, standing firm in the faith because you know that your brothers (and sisters) throughout the world are undergoing the same kind of sufferings. And the God of all grace, who called you to his eternal glory in Christ after you have suffered for a while will himself restore you and make you strong, firm and steadfast" (1 Peter 5:8–10).

Wisdom is a strength that must be practiced. Let God teach you today so you can grow in that strength.

Day 17

Psalm 119:129–136

Your statutes are wonderful;
therefore, I obey them.
The unfolding of your words gives light;
it gives understanding to the simple.
I open my mouth and pant,
longing for your commands.
Turn to me and have mercy on me,
as you always do to those who love your name.
Direct my footsteps according to your word;
let no sin rule over me.
Redeem me from human oppression,
that I may obey your precepts.
Make your face shine on your servant
and teach me your decrees.
Streams of tears flow from my eyes,
for your law is not obeyed.

Question of the day:

What does it mean for God's Word to "unfold?"

1. God's Word gives light.
2. God's Word gives understanding to the simple.
3. God's Word gives me a longing (craving) for more.

4. God's Word allows God to turn to me and grant me mercy.
5. God's Word directs my footsteps so that sin doesn't rule over me.
6. God's Word redeems me from oppression.
7. God's Word teaches me.
8. God's Word makes me hurt for those who don't obey His Law.

When God's Word "unfolds" for me, there is so much to take in. There are stories to be read, wisdom to be gathered throughout. Redeeming love flows from the beginning to the end. There is not a day that I can say that scripture didn't show me something new because even if I had read a piece of scripture before, my circumstance in life may show me something new to apply to my life for the day. There is a reason why scripture says it's active and living because even through it was written so long ago, it still applies to today and into the future.

When I think of verse 130, "it gives understanding to the simple," it makes me think of my husband's preaching. He has such a way of making the most complicated piece of scripture into something a nine-year-old and a ninety-nine-year-old can understand and use at the same time. He has a gift for that. I am blessed to be able to glean from him when I have questions about something in scripture. I say all that because if you are in His Word, He will put people in your path to help shed light on what doesn't make sense. He will teach you and guide you in the right path, and sometimes, that understanding is given to you by others. Look at Daniel or Joseph. Rulers came to them because they knew that they could bring to light what was so confusing to them. If you struggle over understanding God's Word, seek out your pastor or a reputable commentary to help "give light" to what can't be seen. God will direct your steps if you seek Him with all your heart.

Crave His Word today. Let Him redeem your life.

Day 18

Psalm 119:137–144

You are righteous, LORD,
and your laws are right.
The statutes you have laid down are righteous;
they are fully trustworthy.
My zeal wears me out,
for my enemies ignore your words.
Your promises have been thoroughly tested,
and your servant loves them.
Though I am lowly and despised,
I do not forget your precepts.
Your righteousness is everlasting
and your law is true.
Trouble and distress have come upon me,
but your commands give me delight.
Your statutes are always righteous;
give me understanding that I may live.

Question of the day:

What is the difference in living in righteousness and living under the scrutiny of the world?

Living under Scrutiny	Living under Righteousness
1. Enemy ignores your words (v. 139). 2. Lowly and despised (v. 141) 3. Trouble and distress come my way (v. 143). 4. You become a slave to fear (v. 143). 5. Live in a world of sin and suffering (Romans 8:22).	1. God's Word is fully trustworthy (v. 138). 2. His promises have been thoroughly tested, and your servant loves them (v. 140). 3. God's righteousness is everlasting and true (v. 142). 4. Brings me delight and understanding (v. 143–144). 5. We are sons and daughters of God (Romans 8:16). 6. We have to share in His suffering to share in His glory (Romans 8:17). 7. The Spirit intercedes for those that can't find the words to pray (Romans 8:26).

As I read these two lists, it's easy to see the extreme difference. Scrutiny is a world of being beaten down to where you just want to give up. Righteousness is a world where there is faith, hope, love, trust, promises held, delight, inheritance into heaven, and so much more. But it's not an easy ticket. There will be suffering and pain. There will be heartbreak and hurt feelings, but through it all, you are given strength and endurance to push through. The difference between scrutiny and righteousness is God Himself. If you live in the world and by the world's standards, when troubles come your way, then you fold to the pressure. If you live in God and His standards, He is the one that holds you up when you want to fall. He is with you on the darkest of nights reminding you of the bright future ahead.

When we are living under the scrutinizing eyes of others, they only see what's in front of them. But, while they scrutinize, hold fast to God's righteousness so that you can continue to do what God has called you to do. If they don't see your faithfulness to your calling, that's okay because God sees and knows and will hold true to His promises for you. His righteousness has stood the test of time. Those that live for their own agenda have fallen time and time again. God will reign supreme. Stay faithful and focused.

Day 19

Psalm 119:145–160

I call with all my heart; answer me, Lord,
and I will obey your decrees.
I call out to you; save me
and I will keep your statutes.
I rise before dawn and cry for help;
I have put my hope in your word.
My eyes stay open through the watches of the night,
that I may meditate on your promises.
Hear my voice in accordance with your love;
preserve my life, Lord, according to your laws.
Those who devise wicked schemes are near,
but they are far from your law.
Yet you are near, Lord,
and all your commands are true.
Long ago I learned from your statutes
that you established them to last forever.
Look on my suffering and deliver me,
for I have not forgotten your law.
Defend my cause and redeem me;
preserve my life according to your promise.
Salvation is far from the wicked,
for they do not seek out your decrees.
Your compassion, Lord, is great;
preserve my life according to your laws.

Many are the foes who persecute me,
but I have not turned from your statutes.
I look on the faithless with loathing,
for they do not obey your word.
See how I love your precepts;
preserve my life, Lord, in accordance with your love.
All your words are true;
all your righteous laws are eternal.

Question of the day:

How can you shift your thinking during adversity?

1. I call on Him, He answers me, I obey His decrees (v. 145).
2. I call out to Him, He saves me, I keep His statutes (v. 146).
3. I rise before dawn to cry for help, He helps me, I put my hope in Him (v. 147).
4. My eyes stay open through the night to meditate on His Word (v. 148).
5. God hears my voice, He preserves my life, He stays near, and I learn from His statutes (v. 149, 152).
6. I suffer, God delivers me, I don't forget His Law (v. 153).
7. He defends me, He redeems me, He preserves my life (v. 154).
8. His compassion is great toward me; He preserves my life (v. 156).
9. I take notice of the ones that persecute me and are faithless and do not obey God's Word, yet in the midst of them, I still love His precepts, and I know His Word is true and His Laws are eternal (v. 157–160).

It was fascinating to read this as I noticed shifts in thinking. David saw the enemies come, but he also saw God at work at the same time. If he cried out to God, then God actively worked. Since David was so close to God in his relationship, he was able to see past the trouble and see God working. If you look back over the list or the scripture, there is a give and take that happens throughout. God wants to see your faithfulness to Him in the midst of adversity. It's not that He can't save you from your troubles without you asking because He can. However, if you cry out to Him, then you are more likely going to take notice of what He does, and then you can offer Him praise through it all.

God is actively working every day in our midst, but we are so busy or so distracted by life that we don't see Him protecting us from one thing or another. Calling out to God in times of adversity is more for our benefit than it is for His. It is the same with prayer in general. Prayer doesn't change God's mind, but it makes us aware of His working in and around us. And then prayer changes us. It shifts our thinking from me, me, me to God. Our thinking goes from "woe is me" to "thank You, God!"

We are living in difficult times now, but if you are aware and focused on God, you can see Him working and what He is doing is good. He is faithful and just. He calls us to be faithful as well. Open your eyes to what God is doing today.

Day 20

Psalm 119:161–176

Rulers persecute me without cause,
but my heart trembles at your word.
I rejoice in your promise
like one who finds great spoil.
I hate and detest falsehood
but I love your law.
Seven times a day I praise you
for your righteous laws.
Great peace have those who love your law,
and nothing can make them stumble.
I wait for your salvation, LORD,
and I follow your commands.
I obey your statutes,
for I love them greatly.
I obey your precepts and your statutes,
for all my ways are known to you.
May my cry come before you, LORD;
give me understanding according to your word.
May my supplication come before you;
deliver me according to your promise.
May my lips overflow with praise,
for you teach me your decrees.
May my tongue sing of your word,
for all your commands are righteous.

May your hand be ready to help me,
for I have chosen your precepts.
I long for your salvation, LORD,
and your law gives me delight.
Let me live that I may praise you,
and may your laws sustain me.
I have strayed like a lost sheep.
Seek your servant,
for I have not forgotten your commands.

Question of the day:

What does praise and worship look like to those who believe?

1. Persecutors come but I only tremble at God's Word.
2. Rejoice in the promises like finding lost treasure.
3. Lies are hated so we cling to Your Word.
4. Praises rise to God all day because of His righteous laws.
5. Praise includes waiting for His salvation, and while we wait, we follow His commands.
6. Obedience is key because we love His Law and He makes it known to us.

What does praise and worship include?

1. We cry out for understanding.
2. We ask for deliverance because of His promises.
3. Our lips overflow with praise as He teaches us His decrees.
4. Our tongue sings scripture because His words are righteous.
5. We are always ready to receive God's hand of help.
6. We long for His salvation because His Law brings delight.
7. His Law sustains us as we live and praise Him.
8. When we stray, He seeks us like a lost sheep because we are His.

Praise and worship are a vital part of living in God. The way music brings focus back to Him and realigns our thoughts and minds is incredible. On days I have struggled to stay focused at work, it changes completely when my music comes on. Praise music brings peace and comfort on the darkest of days. It also brings even more joy on the happiest of days. It doesn't take away from any celebration but adds to it.

God is God and greatly to be praised. I wrote a song a few years ago that encompasses praise of God because when you think of God, you can't help to lift your voice and offer Him all your praise. Here's the first verse of it:

> I will lift my voice for the glory of my Lord
> I will offer You all of my praise, all of my praise
> For You are glorious, Almighty, marvelous, amazing
> I will lift my voice for the glory of my Lord.

He is the lifter of my head. He is the lover of my soul. He is the bright and morning star. He is everything from beginning to end. He gives us His guide book to follow. In everything, praise Him because He is worthy.

And then *live*!

About the Author

Ann L. Knopp grew up in Tennessee, but when she went to Southern Seminary in Louisville, Kentucky, and met her husband, Faron, Kentucky quickly became her home. She is a woman who wears many hats from being a pastor's wife to a mother of two college sons to working at the community college to ministering to the women in her church and community. She has a passion for sharing God's Word with women through encouragement, teaching, and writing. This book has been a passion project for several years, and she is thrilled to be able to share it with her readers.

CPSIA information can be obtained
at www.ICGtesting.com
Printed in the USA
LVHW031203240621
691050LV00004B/170

9 781098 096335